NATIONAL GEOGRAPHIC
OUR WORLD
STUDENT'S BOOK 2

SERIES
JoAnn (Jodi) Crandall
Joan Kang Shin

AUTHOR
Gabrielle Pritchard

Unit 0		2
Unit 1	Fun in Class	8
Unit 2	The World of Weather	24
Unit 3	Fun in the Sun	40
Units 1–3 Review		56
Unit 4	Inside Our House	58
Unit 5	Day by Day	74
Unit 6	How Are You?	90
Units 4–6 Review		106
Unit 7	Amazing Animals	108
Unit 8	The World of Work	124
Unit 9	Let's Eat!	140
Units 7–9 Review		156
Our World song		158
Cutouts		159
Stickers		

NATIONAL GEOGRAPHIC
LEARNING

Australia • Brazil • Mexico • Singapore • United Kingdom • United States

Unit 0

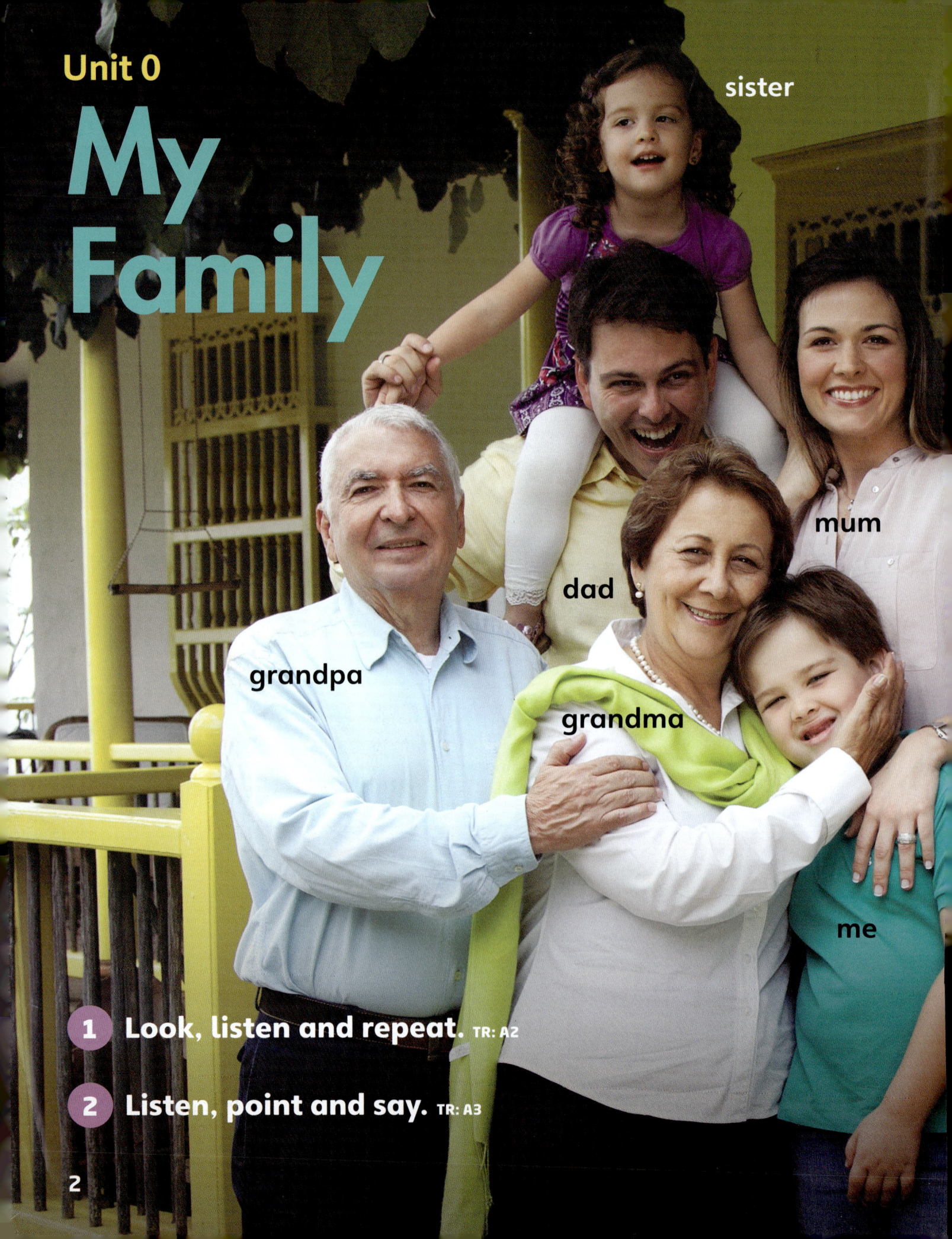

My Family

sister

mum

dad

grandpa

grandma

me

1 Look, listen and repeat. TR: A2

2 Listen, point and say. TR: A3

aunt

cousin

uncle

3 **Work with a friend.** Point. Ask and answer.

Who's that?

It's his cousin!

3

At School

Work in a group.

Be quiet!

Put your hand up.

Hold your card up.

4 **Look, listen and repeat.** TR: A4

5 **Listen, point and say.** TR: A5

Close your book.

Go to the board.

Open your book.

Take out your crayons.

Work with a friend.

6 **Work in a group.** Say and do. Take turns.

Open your books.

5

7 Listen, point and say. TR: A6

I | You | He | She

It | We | You | They

(He = 1)

8 Read and look. Write the number.

1. He's in the kitchen.
2. It's big.
3. You're strong.
4. She's reading.
5. I'm tall.
6. They're my parents.
7. We're friends.
8. You're young.

9 Listen and say. TR: A7

This is **my** teddy bear.

Is this **your** pencil?

It's **his** bike.

Her sandwich looks good.

Its name is Jay-Jay.

This is **our** kite.

That's **your** ball.

It's **their** puzzle.

Numbers

10 **Listen, point and repeat.** TR: A8

11 **Work with a friend.** Point and say.

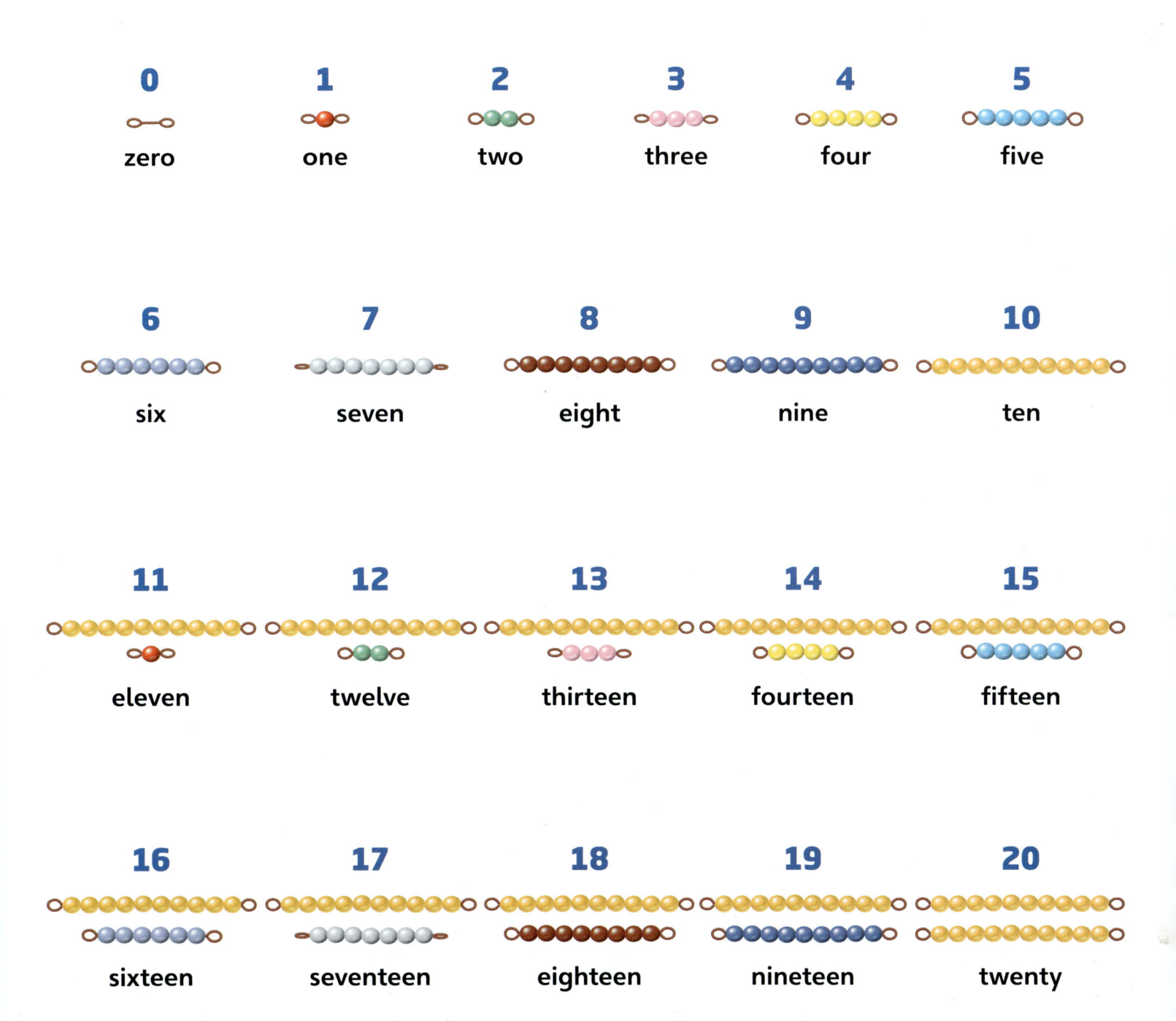

0	1	2	3	4	5
zero	one	two	three	four	five

6	7	8	9	10
six	seven	eight	nine	ten

11	12	13	14	15
eleven	twelve	thirteen	fourteen	fifteen

16	17	18	19	20
sixteen	seventeen	eighteen	nineteen	twenty

Unit 1

Fun in Class

In this unit, I will ...
- say what people are doing.
- say when I use classroom objects.
- show where things are.

Tick T for *True* or F for *Fals*e.

1. The girls are playing. T F
2. The children are having fun. T F
3. They are all wearing white T-shirts. T F

Sack race, Machiques, Venezuela

1 **Listen and say.** TR: A9

2 **Listen, point and say.** TR: A10

reading

counting

colouring

listening

cutting

writing

drawing

gluing

talking

rubbing out

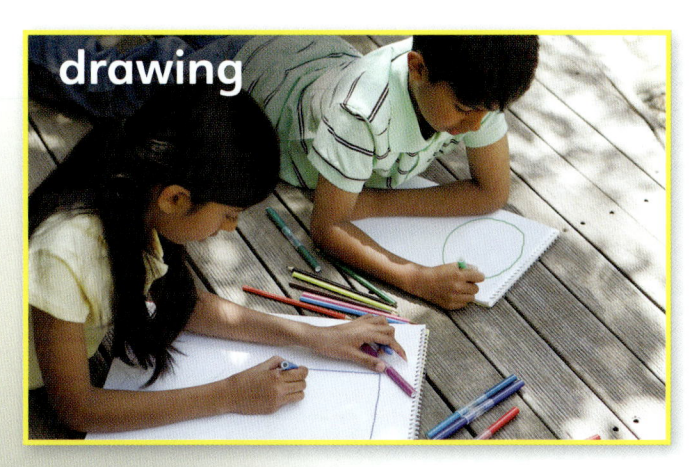

3 **Work with a friend.** Point. Ask and answer.

What are they doing?

They're talking.

11

4 **Listen.** Read and sing. TR: A11

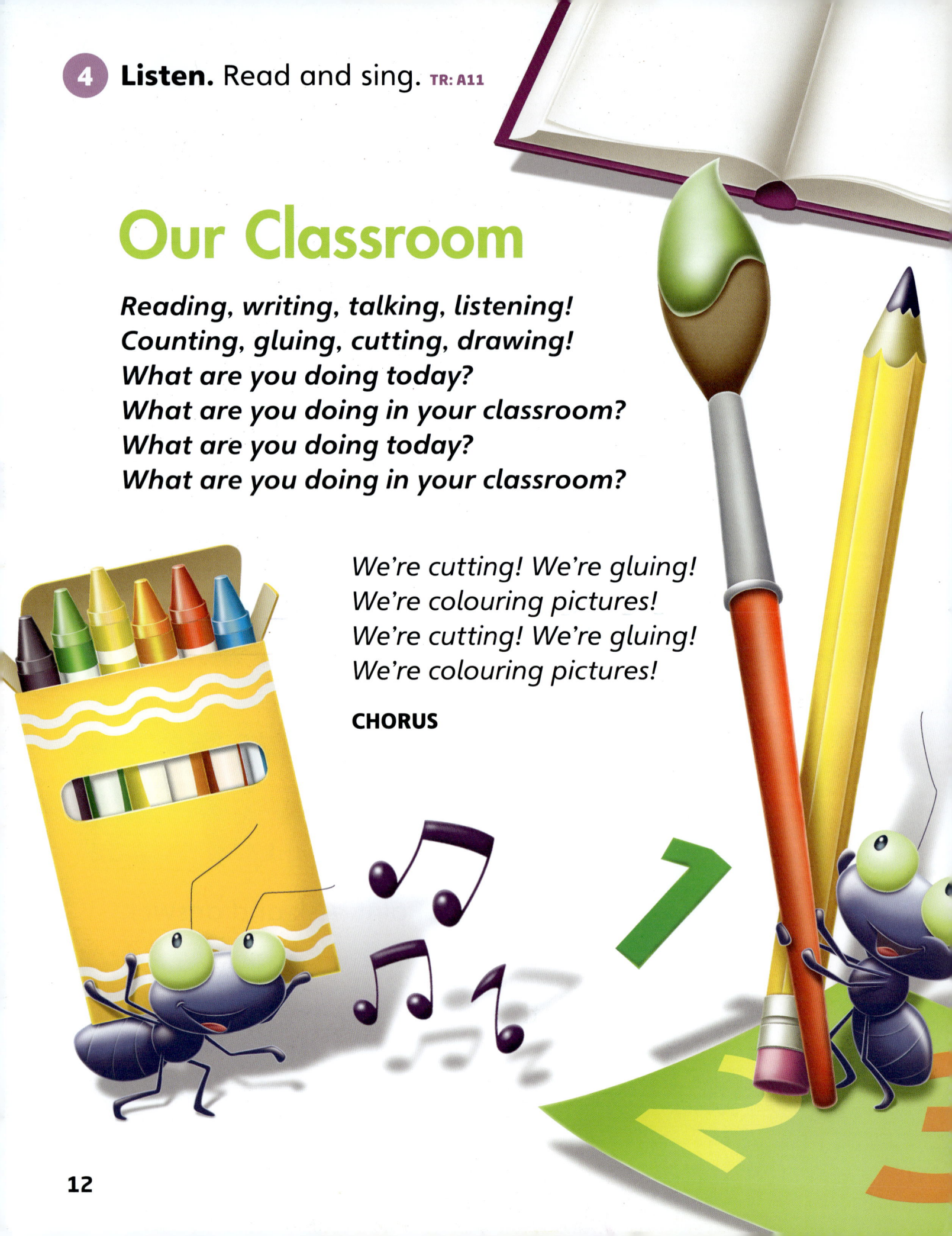

Our Classroom

Reading, writing, talking, listening!
Counting, gluing, cutting, drawing!
What are you doing today?
What are you doing in your classroom?
What are you doing today?
What are you doing in your classroom?

We're cutting! We're gluing!
We're colouring pictures!
We're cutting! We're gluing!
We're colouring pictures!

CHORUS

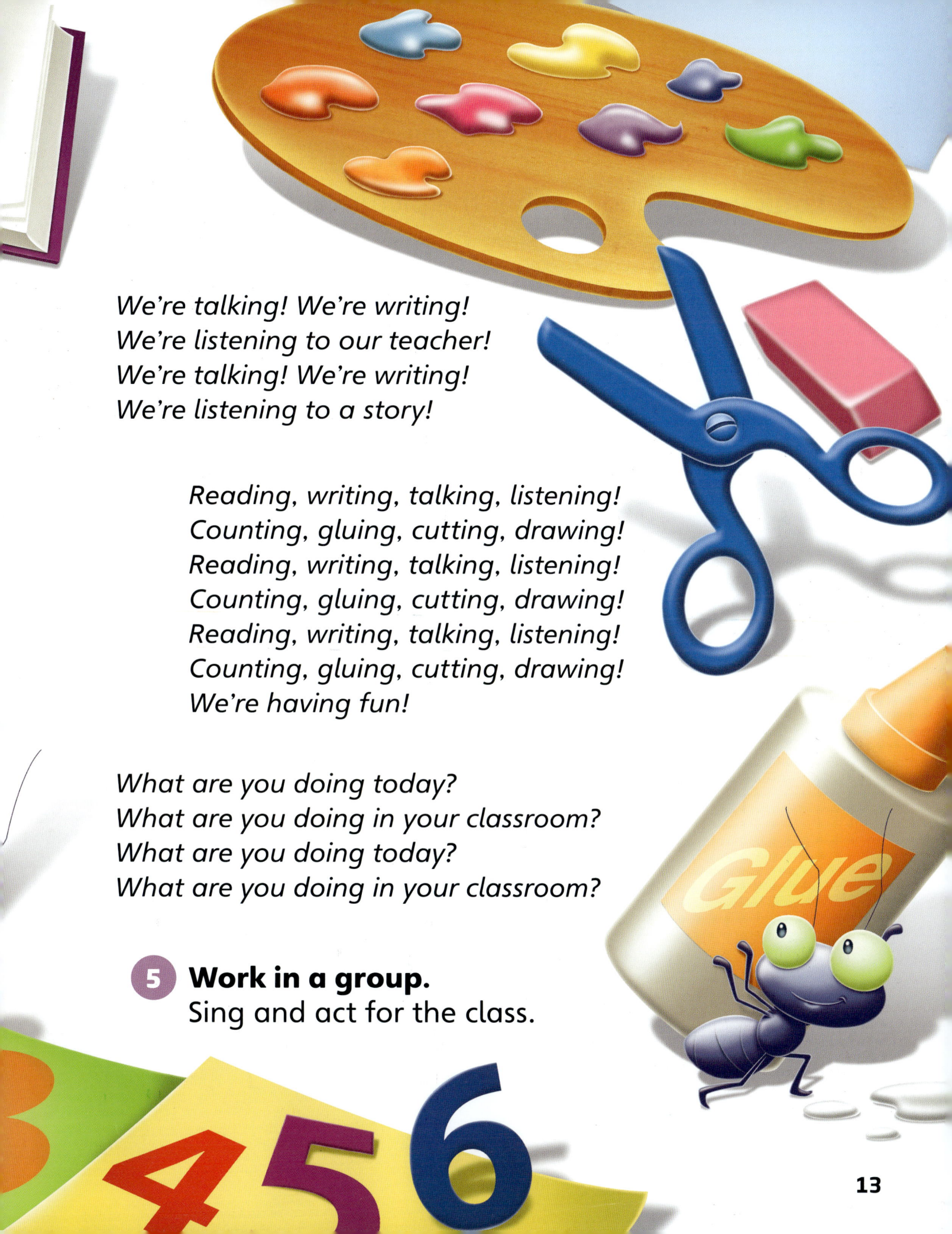

We're talking! We're writing!
We're listening to our teacher!
We're talking! We're writing!
We're listening to a story!

Reading, writing, talking, listening!
Counting, gluing, cutting, drawing!
Reading, writing, talking, listening!
Counting, gluing, cutting, drawing!
Reading, writing, talking, listening!
Counting, gluing, cutting, drawing!
We're having fun!

What are you doing today?
What are you doing in your classroom?
What are you doing today?
What are you doing in your classroom?

5. **Work in a group.**
Sing and act for the class.

GRAMMAR TR: A12

What **are** you **doing**?   We**'re counting** crayons.

6 **Look.** Listen and number the pictures. TR: A13

7 **Look at the ants.** Read and underline.

1. We're painting a picture. / We're drawing a picture.
2. We're talking. / We're rubbing out the numbers.
3. We're listening to a song. / We're listening to a story.
4. We're gluing numbers. / We're gluing shapes.
5. We're colouring circles. / We're cutting paper.
6. We're writing a story. / We're reading a book.

8 **Listen and say.** Read and write. TR: A14

a felt tip

a notebook

glue

a paintbrush

scissors

1. I'm writing. I'm using ___a notebook___.
2. I'm painting. I'm using ___a paintbrush___.
3. I'm drawing. I'm using ___a felt tip___.
4. I'm gluing. I'm using ___glue___.
5. I'm cutting. I'm using ___scissors___.

9 **Listen and stick.** TR: A15

GRAMMAR TR: A16

Are there any felt tips on the table? No, **there aren't**.
Are there any felt tips in the box? Yes, **there are**.

10 **Read.** Look and write.

1. Are there any red paintbrushes on page 15?
   Yes, there are.

2. Are there any scissors on page 10?

3. Are there any notebooks on page 16?

4. Are there any green felt tips on page 8?

5. Are there any pencils on page 13?

11 **Play a game.** Cut out the card on page 159 and colour the pictures. Play with a friend.

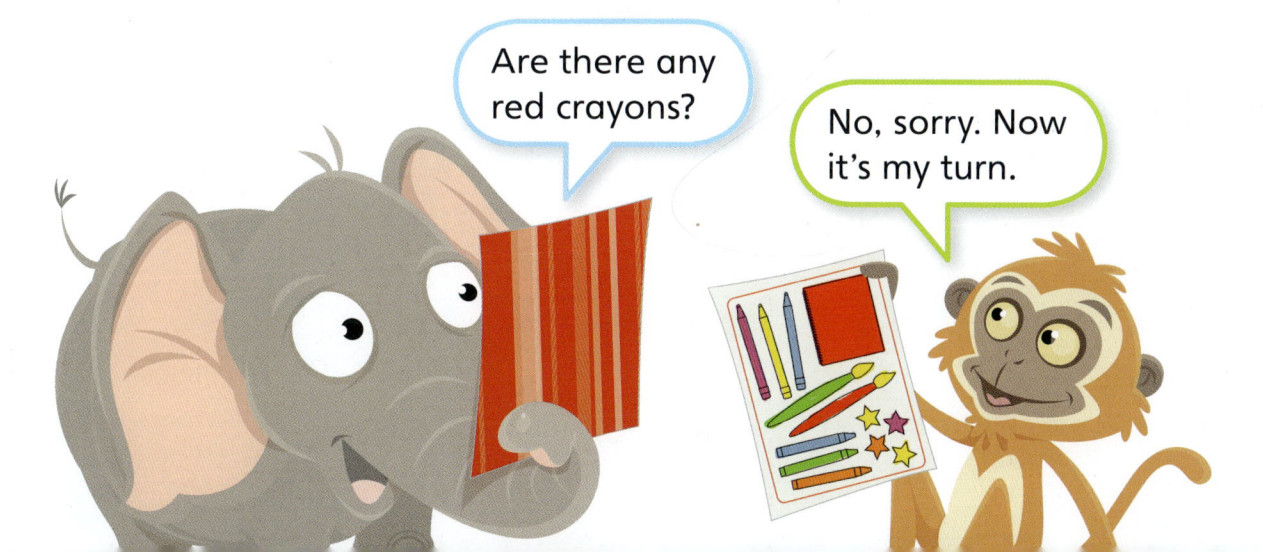

Are there any red crayons?

No, sorry. Now it's my turn.

17

12 **Listen and read.** TR: A17

Paper Art

This girl is making Chinese paper art. She is cutting paper to make a picture of a cat. She is using scissors. Some people make paper animals or flowers. They fold the paper. Then they cut it. Many people put paper art in windows.

In Mexico, people make paper art, too. Look at the paper art below. People cut pictures of flowers, animals and people. They draw a picture and then punch it out. People hang paper art in their houses and outside.

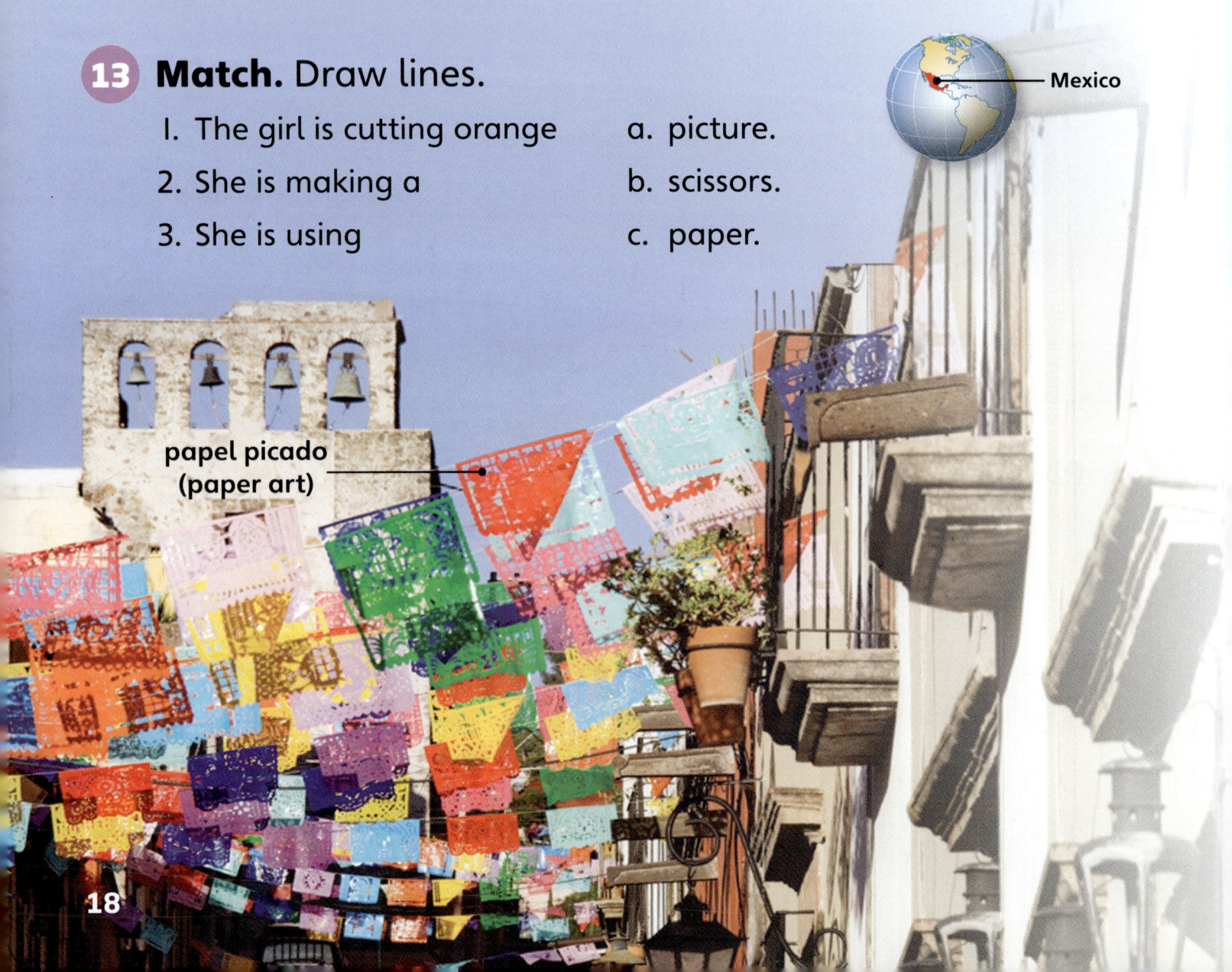

China

13 **Match.** Draw lines.

1. The girl is cutting orange   a. picture.
2. She is making a   b. scissors.
3. She is using   c. paper.

Mexico

papel picado (paper art)

14 **Look and read.** Work with a friend. Talk about paper art.

In China, people
- fold the paper.
- use scissors.
- put the paper art in windows.

In China and Mexico, people
- make paper art.
- make animals and flowers.

In Mexico, people
- do not fold the paper.
- draw the picture.
- hang the paper art in their houses.

15 **Can you find these animals?** Count. Write the number.

__2__ rabbits

__3__ birds

__4__ butterflies

__3__ ducks

Work with a friend. Talk about the picture.

Weird but true
You can fold a piece of paper in half only seven times.

Are there any ducks?

Yes. There are three ducks.

19

This is a picture of Sami and me. We are making a big robot. Sami is cutting shapes. I am gluing paper.

16 **Draw and write.**

Draw a picture of you and your friend.

1. Who is in the picture?

   _____

2. What are you making?

   _____

3. What are you doing?

   _____

17 **Work in groups of three.** Take turns.

Read your writing to your group. Listen. Complete the table about your group.

Name	Action

NATIONAL GEOGRAPHIC

Our World
Be tidy.

18 **Look and read.**

Put your things away.
Be tidy at school and at home.

Classroom, Tokyo, Japan

19 **Read and write.** Talk. What do you put away?

At school I put away _my pencils and my scissors._

At home I put away _____

20 **Make a container for your school supplies.**

1. Draw and cut. 
2. Draw and colour pictures. 
3. Make and glue shapes. 
4. Glue the paper.

Now I can ...
- ○ say what people are doing.
- ○ say when I use classroom objects.
- ○ show where things are.

There are scissors, felt tips and pencils.

23

Unit 2
The World of Weather

In this unit, I will …
- talk about the weather.
- talk about my clothes.
- say when it's hot or cold.

Look and tick.

The girl is wearing
- ◯ a hat.
- ◯ a skirt.
- ◯ gloves.
- ◯ boots.

Girl making a snow angel

1 **Listen and say.** TR: A18

2 **Listen, point and say.** TR: A19

a raincoat

a swimming costume

cloudy

rainy

hot

sunny

boots

26

a jumper

windy

cold

snowy

3 **Work with a friend.**
Point and say. Use the words.

a hat   trousers   boots   gloves
a jumper   a jacket   a raincoat

It's cloudy and rainy.

She's wearing a raincoat and boots.

27

4 **Listen.** Read and sing. TR: A20

Hot or Cold?

Come and look outside.
What can you see?
Today it's snowy.
Put your boots and coat on.
It's cold outside today.

Come and look outside.
What can you see?
Today it's sunny.
Put your trainers and shorts on.
It's hot outside today.

Sledging, Seoul, South Korea

We dress for the weather.
The weather can be hot or cold.
Sometimes it's hot, sometimes it's cold.
Is it hot or cold today?

Take your boots and your jumper off.
Take your hat and your coat off.
What's the weather like?
Is it hot?   Yes!
It's hot outside today.

Put your boots and your jumper on.
Put your hat and your coat on.
What's the weather like?
Is it cold?   Yes!
It's cold outside today.

CHORUS

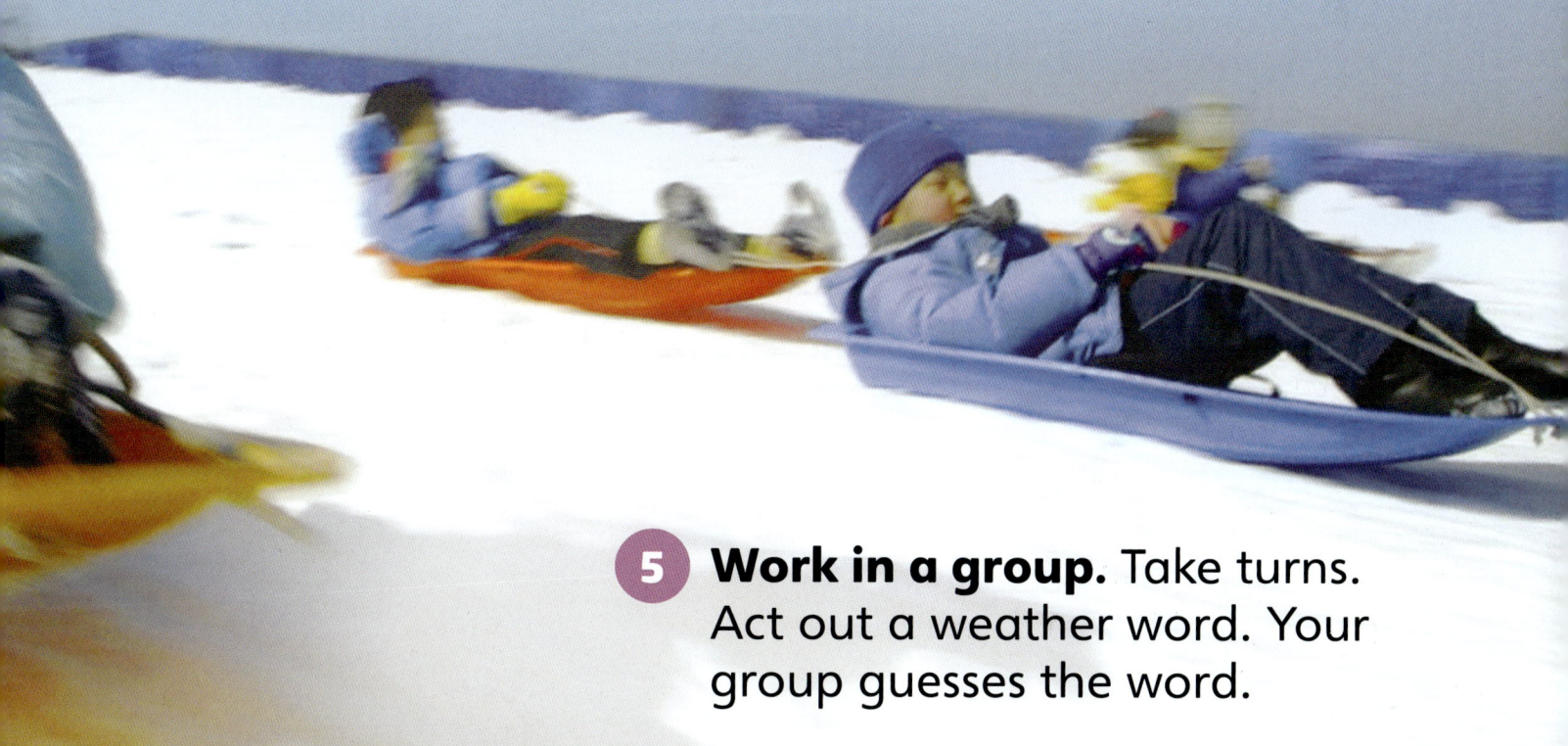

5 **Work in a group.** Take turns. Act out a weather word. Your group guesses the word.

GRAMMAR TR: A21

What's the weather like?   It's windy.

6 What's the weather like? Look, read and write.

1. It's Sunday. _____ It's sunny. _____

2. It's Monday. _____

3. It's Tuesday. _____

4. It's Wednesday. _____

5. It's Thursday. _____

6. It's Friday. _____

Sunday    **Monday**    **Tuesday**

Wednesday    **Thursday**    **Friday**

7 Look and answer.

It's snowy today. What day is it?

It's Tuesday.

30

8 **Work with a friend.** Look at the photos. Talk about the weather.

31

9 **Listen and say.** Look and write. TR: A22

shorts

trainers

an umbrella

a coat

jeans

1. They're _____shorts_____.

2. They're _____.

3. It's _____.

4. It's _____.

5. They're _____.

10 **Talk and stick.** Take turns.

I wear this when it's cold. It's red.

I know! It's a coat!

1   2   3   4   5

32

GRAMMAR TR: A23

It's cold. **Put** your coat **on**.
It's hot. **Take** your jumper **off**.
It's rainy. **Don't forget** your umbrella.

11 Read. Underline the correct answer.

1. It's windy. Put your **dress** / **jacket** on.

2. It's snowy. Don't forget your **boots** / **jeans**.

3. It's sunny. Take your **raincoat** / **trainers** off.

4. It's cold. Don't forget your **umbrella** / **gloves**.

5. It's hot. Put your **coat** / **shorts** on.

12 Play a game. Cut out the cards on page 161. Play with a friend.

It's rainy.

Don't forget your umbrella.

Good. Your turn.

13 Listen and read. TR: A24

Snow Animals

The Arctic is a very cold and snowy place. Arctic animals haven't got winter clothes. Some arctic animals have got thick fur. Their fur keeps them warm. It hides them in the snow.

The polar bear, arctic fox and arctic hare are arctic animals. Polar bears are big, strong animals. The arctic fox and the arctic hare are small, fast animals. The arctic fox and the arctic hare have got white fur in the winter and brown fur in the summer.

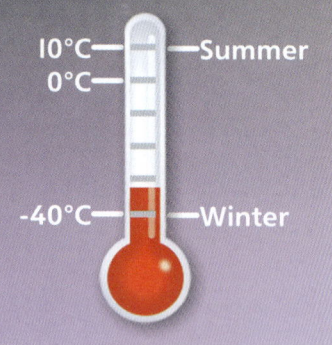

arctic hare   arctic fox

10°C — Summer
0°C
-40°C — Winter

Weird but true: Polar bears are black under their fur.

14 Read. Tick **T** for *True* or **F** for *False*.

1. The Arctic is very hot. (T) (F)
2. Some arctic animals have got thick fur to keep them warm. (T) (F)
3. The arctic fox has got brown fur in the winter. (T) (F)

15 Read and tick.

	Polar bear	Arctic fox	Arctic hare
lives in the Arctic	✓		
is big			
is small			
is strong			
is fast			
has got white fur in the winter			
has got brown fur in the summer			

16 Read and write.

1. The polar bear, arctic fox and arctic hare live in the _____Arctic_____.

2. The polar bear is big and _____.

3. The arctic hare and arctic fox are _____ and fast.

4. The arctic fox and the arctic hare have got _____ fur in the winter.

5. The arctic fox and the arctic hare have got _____ fur in the summer.

17 Which animals live in the Arctic? Work with a friend. Talk about the animals you know.

What about cats?

Cats don't live in the Arctic.

35

In this photo I'm with my friends. We're having fun. It's a hot and sunny day. I'm wearing a red T-shirt, shorts and a sun hat. Can you see me?

18 **Write.** What about you? Find or draw a picture of yourself. Write.

1. Where are you? Who are you with?

   _____

2. What's the weather like?

   _____

3. What are you wearing?

   _____

19 **Work in groups of three.** Take turns. Read your writing to your group. Listen. Complete the table.

Name		
Weather		
Clothes		

NATIONAL GEOGRAPHIC

Our World

Dress for the weather.

20 Look and read. What's the weather like? Look.

Wear the right clothes!

Berguedà, Catalonia, Spain

21 Read and write. Talk. How do you dress for the weather?

1. When it's rainy, I wear a raincoat and boots.
   _____.

2. When it's hot, I wear _____
   _____.

37

22 **Make a weather and clothes mobile.**

1 Draw and cut out weather pictures.

2 Cut out clothes pictures.

3 Put ribbon on a hanger. Add the weather pictures.

4 Add the clothes pictures.

It's cold in winter. I wear my boots, my coat and my gloves.

Now I can ...
- ○ talk about the weather.
- ○ talk about my clothes.
- ○ say when it's hot or cold.

39

Unit 3

Fun in the Sun

In this unit, I will …
- say what I like doing outside.
- say what I do on different days.
- say what I like.

Look and tick.

The children are
- ☐ swimming.
- ☐ running.
- ☐ playing.

Boys playing in the water, Klungkung, Bali

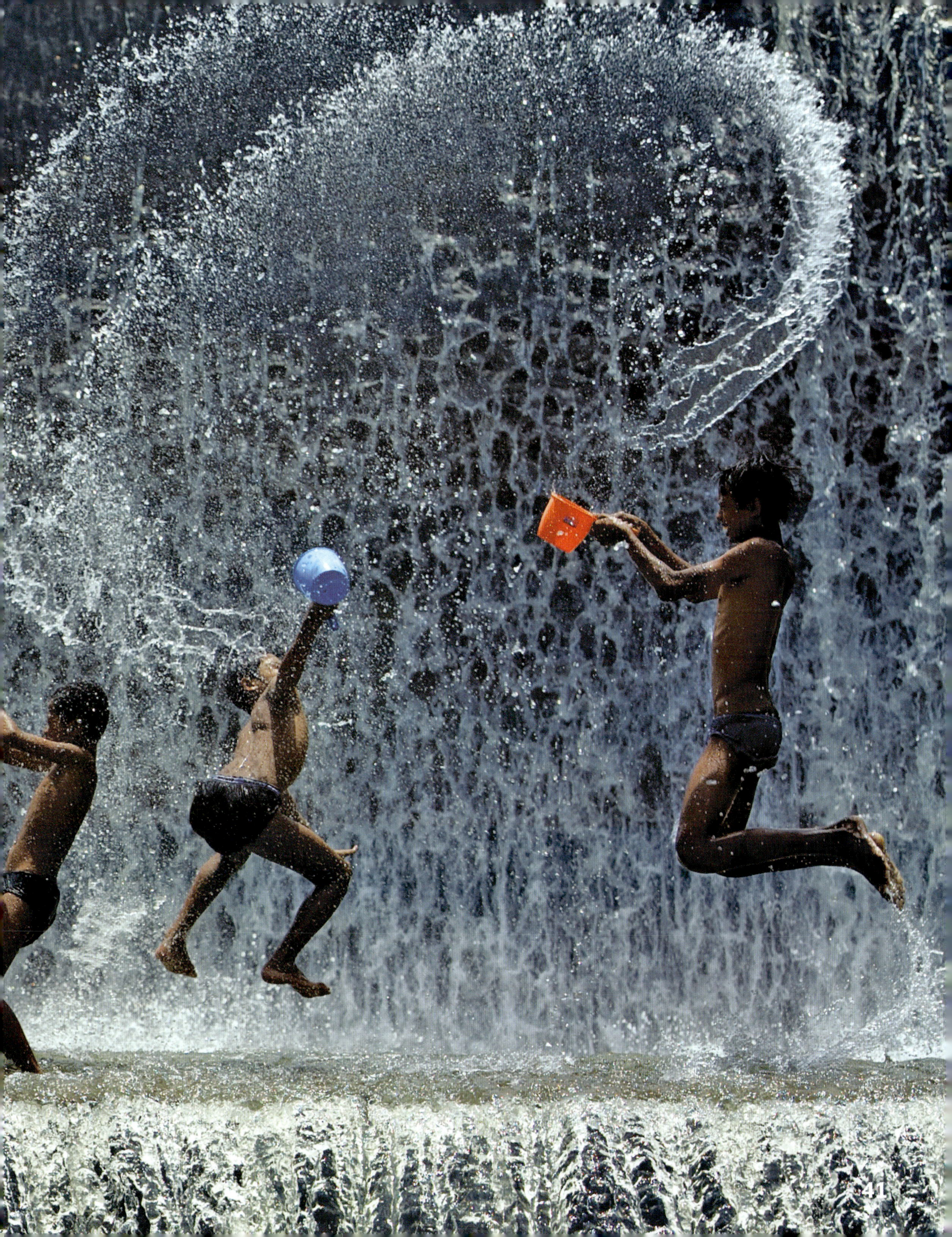

1 **Listen and say.** TR: A25

2 **Listen, point and say.** TR: A26

play a game

skateboard

fly a kite

skip

play hide and seek

ride a bike

rollerblade

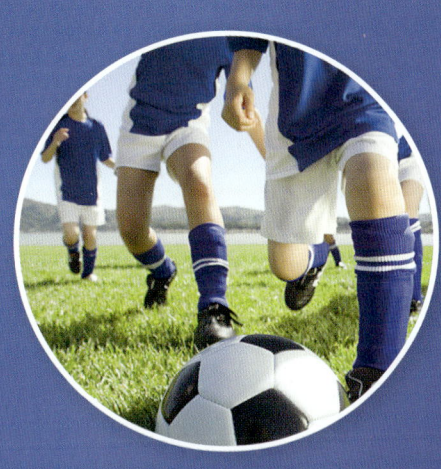

play football

play baseball

play basketball

3 **Work with a friend.** Point. Ask and answer.

What are they doing?

They're playing basketball.

43

4 **Listen.** Read and sing. TR: A27

Outside

Hey! What do you like doing outside?

I like riding a bike.
Yes, I do. Yes, I do.
I like flying a kite.
Yes, I do. Yes, I do.
I like playing games.
I like playing outside with you.
It's fun, fun, fun!

What is fun for you?
What do you like to do?
Do you like playing?
Let's play outside all day.

What is fun for you?
What do you like to do?
Do you like playing?
Let's play outside all day.
What is fun for you?

Do you like skateboarding?
No, I don't.
Playing hide and seek?
No, I don't.
Playing basketball?
No. It's boring.

CHORUS

I like skipping.
Yes, I do. Yes, I do.
I like rollerblading.
Yes, I do. Yes, I do.
I like playing football.
I like playing with you.
It's fun, fun, fun!

CHORUS

5 **Work in a group.** Take turns. Act out your favourite activity for your group to guess.

GRAMMAR TR: A28

Do you **like playing** baseball?   Yes, I do. It's fun.
Do you **like skipping**?   No, I don't. It's boring.

6 **What about you?** Answer.

1. Do you like playing baseball? _____
2. Do you like rollerblading? _____
3. Do you like playing hide and seek? _____
4. Do you like riding a bike? _____
5. Do you like skateboarding? _____

GRAMMAR TR: A29

| What do you **like doing**? | I **like playing** baseball. |
| What do they **like doing**? | They **like skipping**. |

7 **Work in a group of three.** Take turns. Ask and answer. Tell the class about your group.

What do you like doing?

I like swimming.

47

8 **Listen and say.** TR: A30

bounce a ball

throw a ball

catch a ball

watch a game

play tag

9 **Read.** Look at the pictures. Match.

1. I like bouncing a ball. __a__
2. They like playing tag. _____
3. I like throwing a ball. _____
4. I like catching a ball. _____
5. I like watching a game. _____

10 **Say and stick.** Work with a friend.

Do you like playing tag?

No. It's boring.

1   2   3   4   5

48

GRAMMAR TR: A31

Let's throw a ball. Yes! That sounds like fun! 🙂
Let's bounce a ball. No, thanks. 🙁

11 **Read, write and draw.** What do you think?

1. _Let's play_ football. → 🙁
2. _____ a game. →
3. _____ a ball. →
4. _____ hide and seek. →
5. _____ tag. →

12 **Play a game.** Cut out the pictures and the cube on page 163. Glue. Play with a friend.

Let's skip.

Yes! That sounds like fun!

49

13 Listen and read. TR: A32

A Big Ball of Fun

These girls are in special balls. The balls are very big and very strong. Some balls have got water inside them.

Moving in a ball is fun and exciting. You climb inside. Then you walk or run and the ball rolls. It can roll very fast. Sometimes it bounces, too. You can run in a ball downhill or on water.

Lots of people like doing this. It's fast, fun and exciting!

14 Match. Draw lines.

1. Balls roll very
2. Sometimes balls
3. You can ride balls on

a. water.
b. fast.
c. bounce.

15 **What can you do in a ball?** Write.

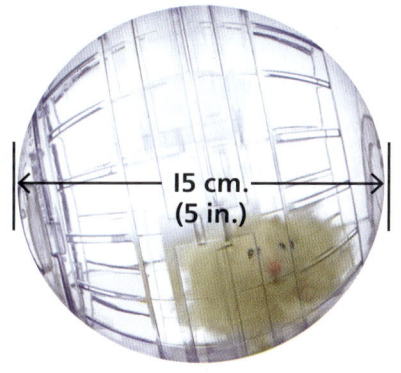

crawl

Hamsters run in balls, too!

16 **Work with a friend.** How many kinds of balls can you name?

51

At home I like skateboarding. At school I like playing hide and seek. It's fun. On Saturdays I like playing basketball with my friends.

17 **Write.** Write about what you like doing.

1. What do you like doing at home?
   _____

2. What do you like doing at school?
   _____

3. What do you like doing on Saturdays?
   _____

18 **Work in groups of three.** Take turns. Read your writing to your group. Listen. Complete the table.

Name	At home	At school	On Saturdays

NATIONAL GEOGRAPHIC

Our World

Be a good sport.

19 **Look and read.**

Play by the rules. Be fair and take turns. Have fun!

20 **Read and write.** Talk.

How do you play fairly?

We _take turns._

21 **Make a mural.** Draw what you do outside.

1 Put the paper on the wall.

2 Draw your picture.

3 Paint your picture.

4 Write your name.

54

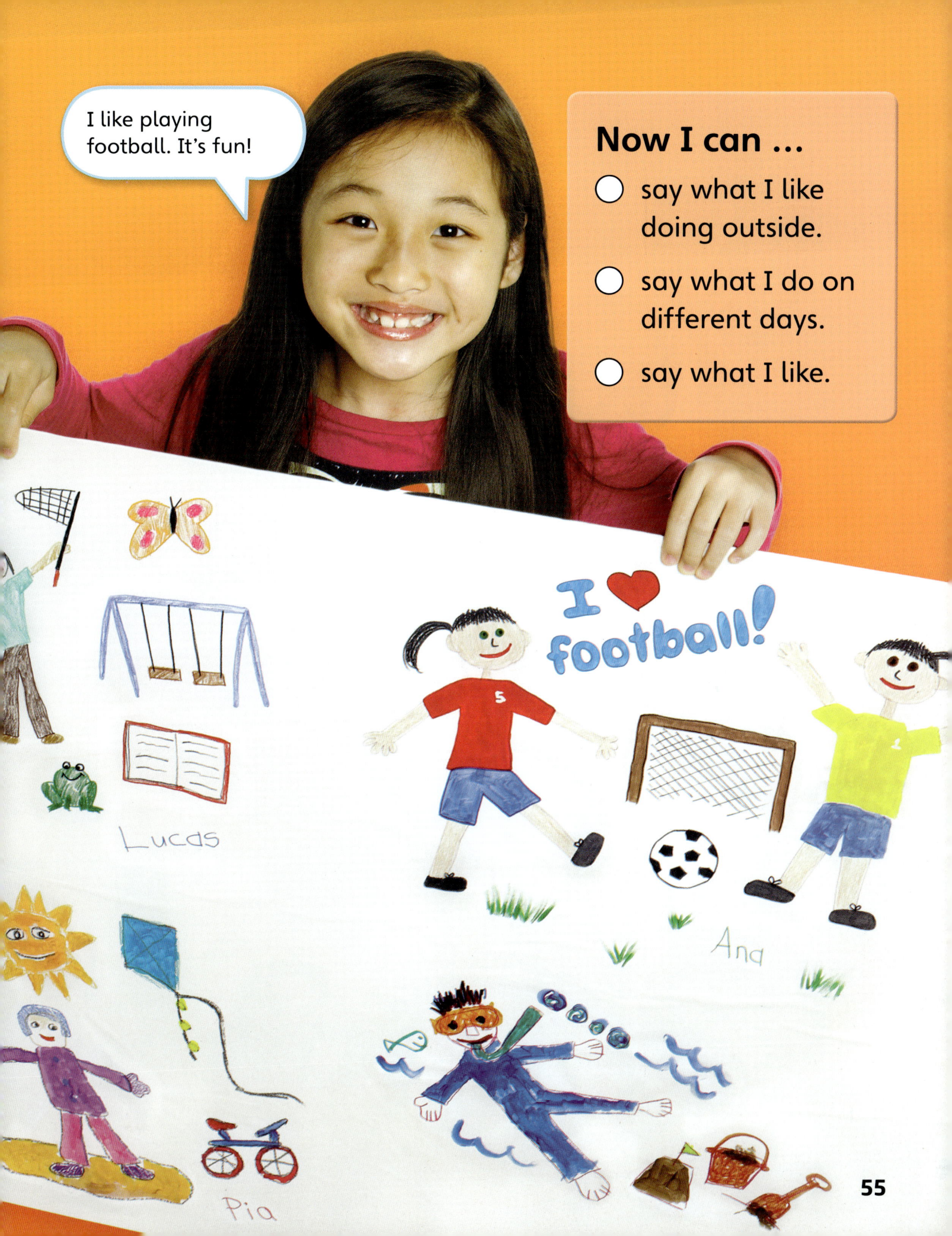

I like playing football. It's fun!

Now I can ...

○ say what I like doing outside.

○ say what I do on different days.

○ say what I like.

I ♥ football!

Lucas

Ana

Pia

55

Review

Start

Hop in a circle.

Sing your favourite song.

56

You forgot your gloves. Go back one space.

Work in groups. Look and play. Ask and answer.

Do you like skateboarding?

Yes, I do.

Finish

57

Unit 4

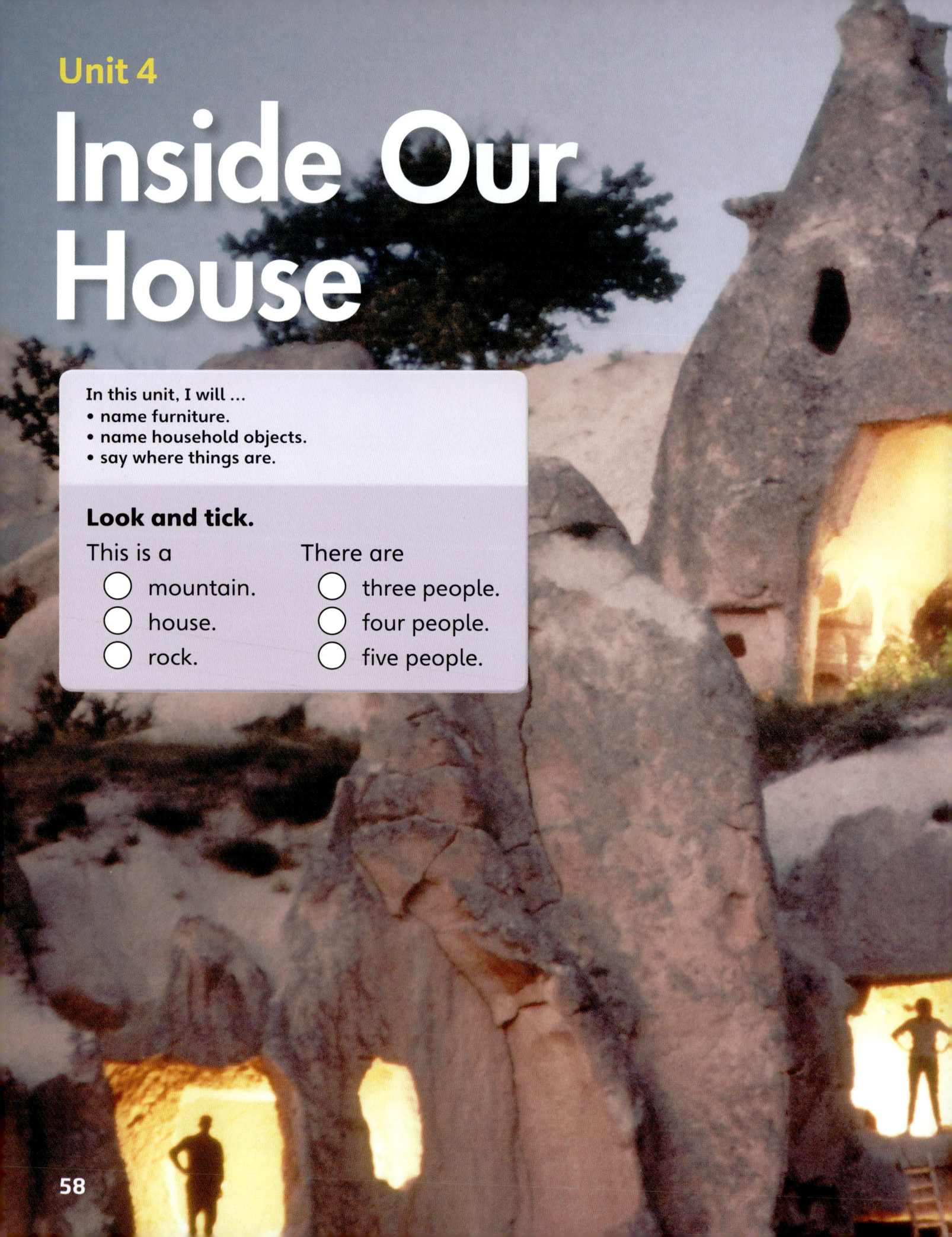

Inside Our House

In this unit, I will ...
- name furniture.
- name household objects.
- say where things are.

Look and tick.

This is a
- ◯ mountain.
- ◯ house.
- ◯ rock.

There are
- ◯ three people.
- ◯ four people.
- ◯ five people.

58

Cave house, Cappadocia, Turkey

1 **Listen and say.** TR: A33

2 **Listen, point and say.** TR: A34

a microwave

a bath

a cooker

shelves

60

3 **Work with a friend.**
Ask and answer.

- a shower
- stairs
- a bookcase
- a fireplace
- a rug
- an armchair

Is there a fireplace in the living room?

Yes, there is.

61

4 **Listen.** Read and sing. TR: A35

My House

*Welcome to my house.
This is where I live.
Welcome to my living room.
Is there a place to sit?*

*The armchair is in front of the fireplace.
Sit down and warm your feet.
The fireplace is next to the bookcase.
Let's find a book to read.*

*Welcome to my house.
This is where I live.
Welcome to my kitchen.
Is there food in there?*

*The fridge is between the windows.
There's lots of food inside.
Something's cooking on the cooker.
May I try some? May I, please?*

**Welcome to my house.
This is where I live.
Welcome to my bedroom.
Is there a place to sleep?**

My pillow is on my bed.
It's where I put my head.
I turn off the light above me.
And then I go to sleep.

Where is the fireplace? It's in the living room.
Where is the cooker? It's in the kitchen.
Where is the light? It's in the bedroom.

**Welcome to my house.
This is where I live.
It was nice to see you.
Please come again!
Welcome to my house!**

5 **Sing again.** Hold up pictures.

GRAMMAR TR: A36

above

behind

in front of

between

next to

under

6 **Work with a friend.** Read to each other. Tick **T** for *True* or **F** for *False*.

1. The red butterfly is between the flowers. T ✓
2. The purple butterfly is under the bush. T F
3. The yellow butterfly is next to the tree. T F
4. The green butterfly is above the flower. T F
5. The blue butterfly is behind the bush. T F
6. The orange butterfly is above the flowers. T F

7 **Look and write.**

1. The fireplace is _under the mirror_.

2. The table is _____.

3. The rug is _____.

4. The shelves are _____.

5. The armchair is _____.

6. The bookcase is _____.

8 **Listen and say.** Look and write. TR: A37

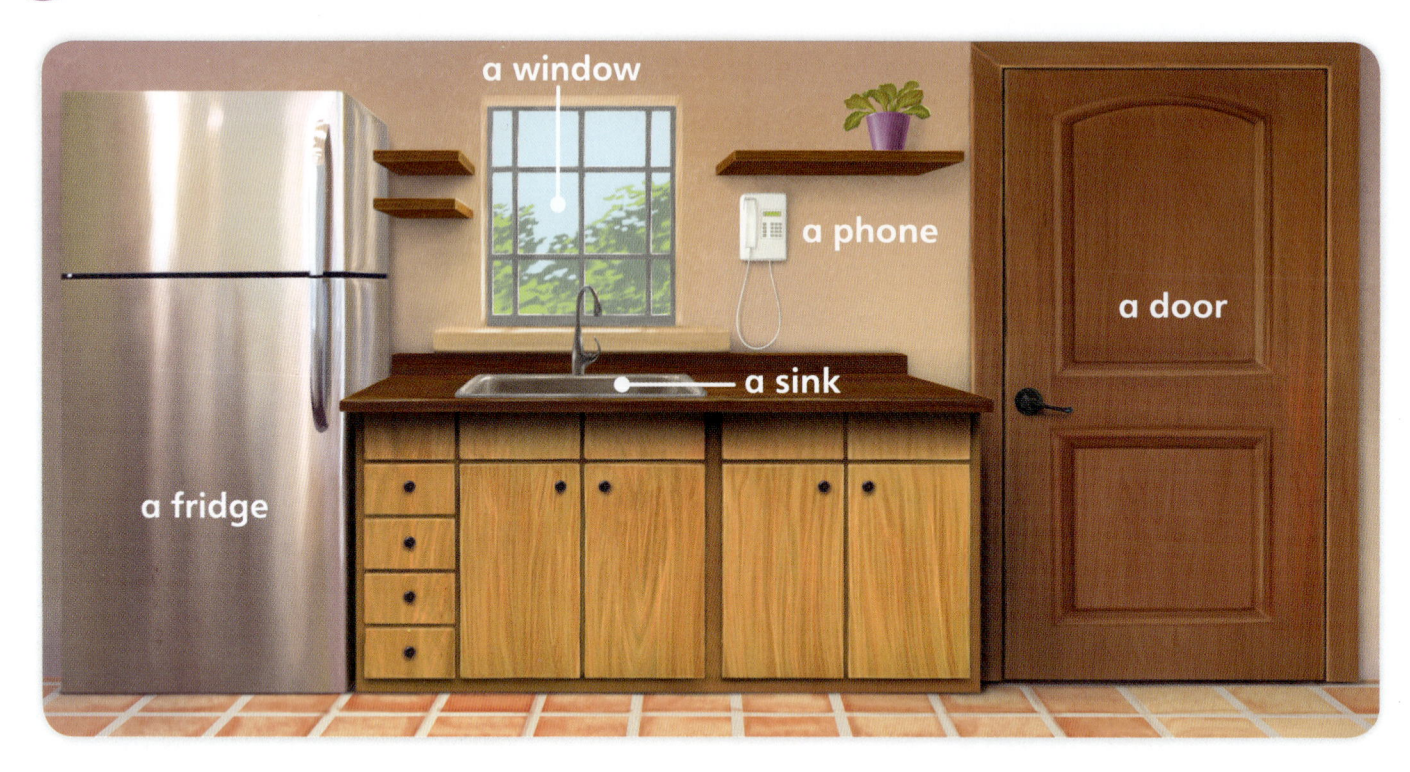

a window
a phone
a door
a sink
a fridge

1. There are two shelves between the _____
   and the _____.

2. There is a _____ under the big shelf.

3. There is a window above the _____.

4. The plant is next to the _____.

9 **Listen and stick.** Compare your answers. TR: A38

Where's the phone? It's on the shelf.

behind   between   next to   under   on

66

GRAMMAR TR: A39

| Where's the **phone**? | **It**'s in the kitchen. |
| Where are the **lamps**? | **They**'re in the living room. |

10 **Play a game.** Look and remember. Play with a friend.

Where are the armchairs?

They're in the kitchen. I think they're in front of the door.

11 **Look at the picture.** Write about the cat, the frogs and the flowers.

67

12 **Listen and read.** TR: A40

Fun Houses

Aeroplane House

Jo-Ann Ussery's house is an aeroplane. It is big and there are lots of windows. Inside there is a living room, a dining room and a kitchen. There are three bedrooms, too. There is even a bathroom with a bath. It is fun to live in an aeroplane!

Egg House

Dai Haifei's house is very small. There is only one room inside. In the room there is a bed, a small table and a lamp. There aren't any chairs. Grass grows on the outside of the house. It is fun to live in a house that is the shape of an egg!

aeroplane house

egg house

AEROPLANE HOUSE
39 m. (127 ft.)

EGG HOUSE
3 m. (10 ft.)

13 Read and match. Draw lines.

1. Dai Haifei's house is the shape of an   aeroplane.
2. His house is very   big.
3. Jo-Ann Ussery's house is an   egg.
4. Her house is   small.

14 Read and write.

1. Is there a kitchen in the egg house? _No, there isn't._

2. Is the egg house big? _____

3. Are there bedrooms in the aeroplane house? _____

4. Are there any chairs in the egg house? _____

5. Is there a bathroom in the aeroplane house? _____

15 Work with a friend. Look and read. Talk about the houses.

Egg House	Aeroplane House
one room table a bed and lamp grass on the outside	seven rooms dining room three bedrooms lots of windows

Weird but true

In this house, everything is upside down!

16 Work with a friend. Talk about your house. Take turns.

69

This is my living room. It's my favourite room. There's a big rug in front of the fireplace. I like doing my puzzles there. There's an armchair next to the sofa. I like sitting on the sofa and watching TV.

17 **Write.** Write about a room in your house.

1. What room are you writing about?

   _____

2. Describe the room and furniture.

   _____

   _____

3. What do you like doing in the room?

   _____

18 **Work in groups of three.** Take turns. Read your writing to your group. Listen. Complete the table.

Name	Room

70

NATIONAL GEOGRAPHIC

Our World

Help at home.

19 **Look and read.**

Help your family.
Help with the chores.

20 **Read.** Talk and write.

How can you help at home?

I can _help in the kitchen._

21 **Make a shoebox house.**

1 Paint and glue boxes.

2 Make rooms.

3 Cut out the pictures on page 165. Glue the pictures.

4 Make furniture and draw more pictures.

Now I can ...
- ○ name furniture.
- ○ name household objects.
- ○ say where things are.

Look! The fridge is next to the cooker.

73

Unit 5

Day by Day

In this unit, I will …
- talk about what I do every day.
- talk about when I do things.
- name parts of the day.

Look and tick.

This animal is
- ⭕ eating.
- ⭕ talking.
- ⊗ having a bath.
- ⭕ sleeping.

Parrot having a bath, Costa Rica

1 **Listen and say.** TR: B2

2 **Listen, point and say.** TR: B3

get up

wash my face

brush my teeth

go to school

have lunch

play with friends

play computer games

3 **Work with a friend.**
Point and say.

I get up. Then I wash my face.

I wash my face. Then I get dressed.

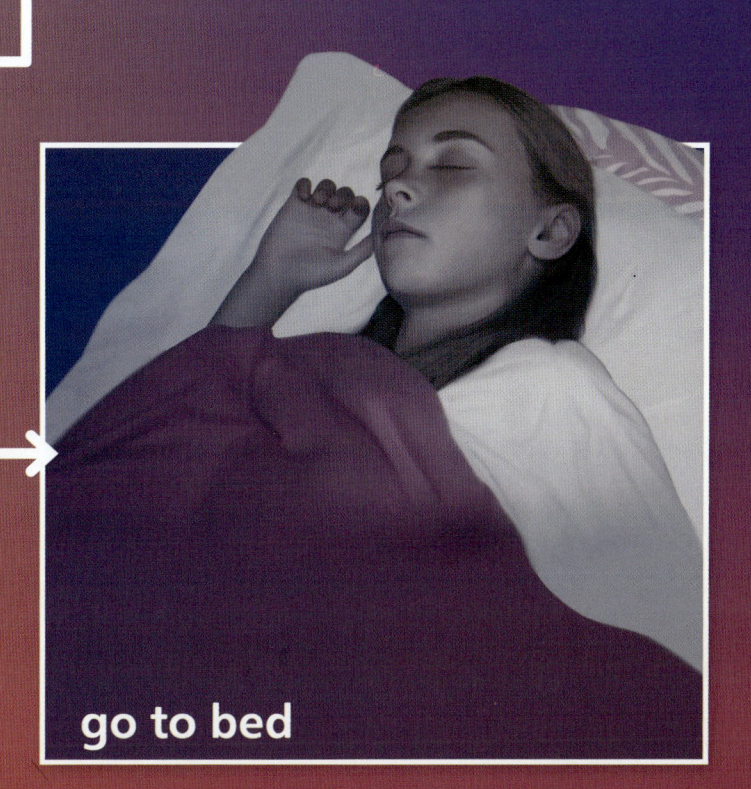

get dressed

have breakfast

have dinner

go to bed

4 **Listen.** Read and sing. TR: B4

Day by Day

*What time is it? What time is it?
What time is it? Can you tell me?*

It's seven o'clock. It's seven o'clock.
It's seven o'clock in the morning.
I always get up at seven o'clock.
I get up at seven every day.

CHORUS

It's eight o'clock. It's eight o'clock.
It's eight o'clock in the morning.
I go to school at eight o'clock.
I always go to school at eight.

CHORUS

It's three o'clock. It's three o'clock.
It's three o'clock in the afternoon.
I always play with friends at three o'clock.
I play with my friends every day.

CHORUS

It's nine o'clock. It's nine o'clock.
It's nine o'clock at night.
I go to sleep at nine o'clock.
I go to sleep at nine every day.

5 **Work in a group.** Take turns. Say a time. Your friends say what they do at that time.

GRAMMAR TR: B5

What time is it?	It's 1.00.	It's one o'clock.
When do you get up?	At 7.00.	At seven o'clock.
When does he go to bed?	At 9.00.	At nine o'clock.

6 **What time is it?** Listen. Look and write. TR: B6

1. It's four o'clock.
2. _____
3. _____
4. _____
5. _____
6. _____

7 **Work with a friend.** Ask and answer.

What time is it?

It's three o'clock.

80

8 **Look and write questions.** Then work with a friend. Ask and answer.

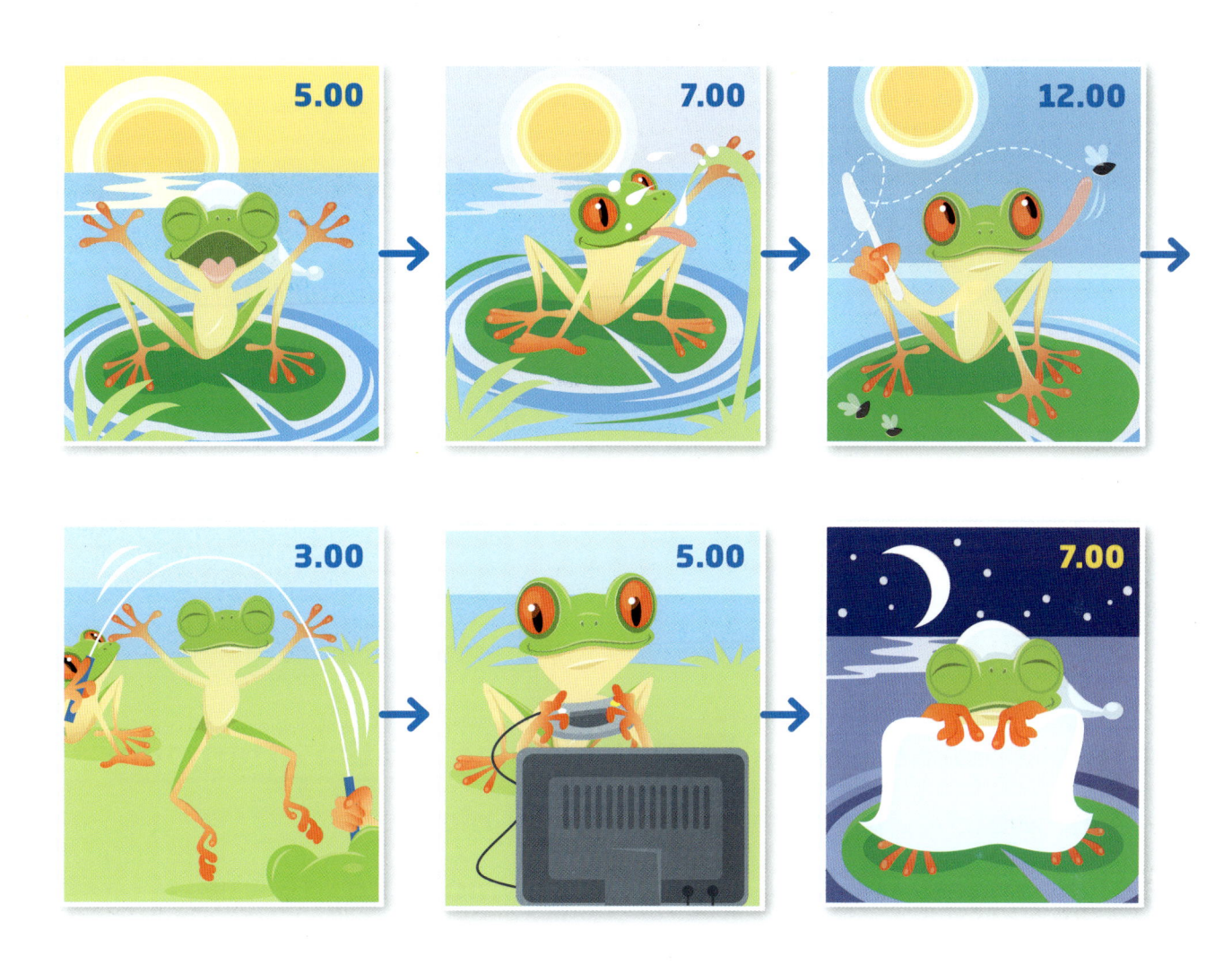

1. get up _____ When does Freddy get up? _____

2. wash his face _____

3. have lunch _____

4. play with friends _____

5. play computer games _____

6. go to bed _____

9 **Listen and say.** Listen. Read and underline. TR: B7

in the morning

late

in the afternoon

in the evening

at night

1. Hana plays basketball **in the morning** / **in the afternoon**.
2. She watches TV **in the evening** / **at night**.
3. Peter rides his bike in the **evening** / **morning**.
4. He plays computer games **at night** / **in the afternoon**.
5. He's **late for school** / **late for dinner**.

10 **Work with a friend.** Say and stick.

When do you play with friends?

In the afternoon.

morning | afternoon | evening | night | Sometimes, I'm late for

82

GRAMMAR TR: B8

What do you do **every day**?   I brush my teeth **every day**.
I **always** read a book in the evening.

What does your brother do on Saturdays?
He sleeps! He **never** gets up before 10 o'clock.

I ride my bike to school every morning.

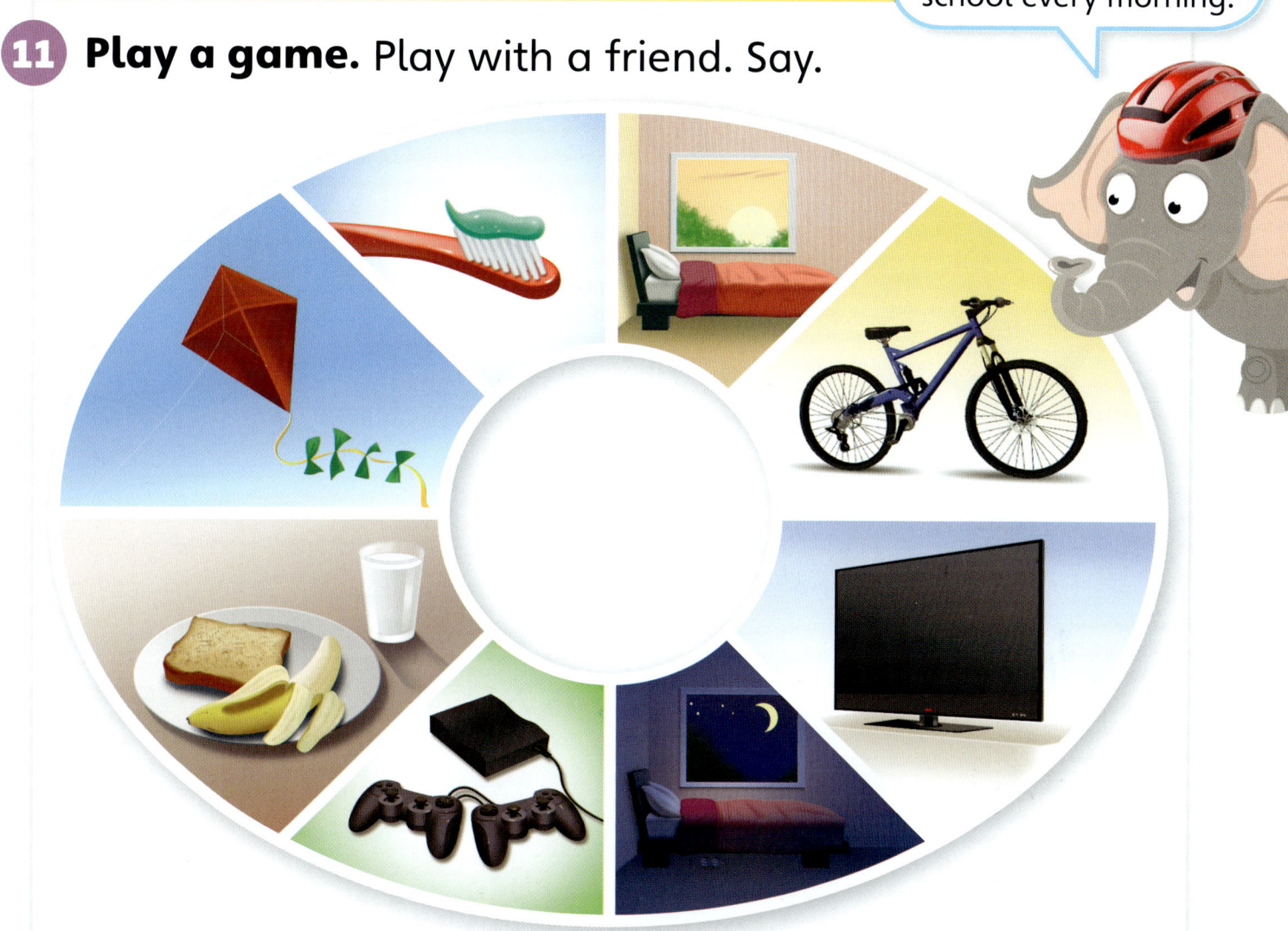

11 **Play a game.** Play with a friend. Say.

12 **Write.** Work in groups of four. Talk about your friend.

My friend always _____.

_____ never _____.

_____ every day.

83

13 **Listen and read.** TR: B9

A Day in the Space Station

Astronauts at the International Space Station are busy all day. They get up at seven o'clock. Then they wash and have breakfast. At eight o'clock, they start experiments. In the morning they also exercise for an hour.

At one o'clock, the astronauts have lunch. The food is prepared on Earth and put in special bags. The astronauts can choose from over a hundred different foods. In the afternoon the astronauts do more experiments. Sometimes they put on a space suit and space walk outside. They exercise for another hour, too.

At seven o'clock, they have dinner. In the evening the astronauts read, send emails or take photos of space. At about ten o'clock, they go to bed.

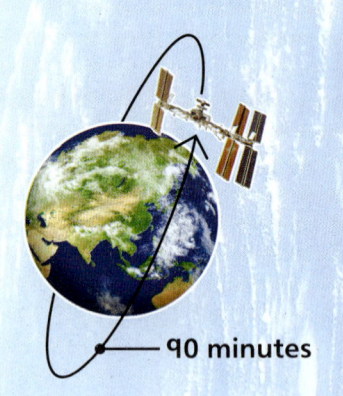

90 minutes

have lunch

go to bed

14 **Read and look.** Tick **T** for *True* or **F** for *False*.

1. Astronauts aren't busy in the morning. T F
2. Space food is prepared on Earth. T F
3. The space station circles the Earth in 90 minutes. T F

15 **Read and write.** Work with a friend. Talk about a day in the space station.

Morning

- get up at _7 o'clock_ • wash and have _____
- start experiments at _____ • exercise for _____ hour

⬇

Afternoon

- have lunch at _____ • do more _____
- sometimes they space _____ • exercise for _____ hour

⬇

Evening

- have dinner at _____ • read, send emails or take _____
- go to bed at _____

16 **Work with a friend.** Answer the questions.

1. When do astronauts exercise?
2. What time do they start experiments?
3. When do astronauts space walk?
4. When do they read?
5. What time do the astronauts go to bed?

Weird but true

Astronauts grow about 5 cm. (2 in.) in space.

17 **Work with a friend.** Talk about your day. How is it different from an astronaut's day? How is it similar?

The astronauts get up at seven o'clock.

I get up at seven o'clock, too. What about you?

85

My favourite day is Saturday. I never have breakfast before 10 o'clock in the morning. I ride my bike or rollerblade with my friends in the afternoon. I play computer games with my sister in the evening. Saturday is always a great day!

18 **Write.** Write about your favourite day.

1. What is your favourite day?

   _____

2. What do you do in the morning?

   _____

3. What do you do in the afternoon?

   _____

4. What do you do in the evening?

   _____

19 **Work in groups of three.** Take turns. Read your writing to your group. Listen. Complete the table.

Name	Favourite day

NATIONAL GEOGRAPHIC

Our World

Be on time.

20 Look and read.

Don't be late.
Plan your day.

Tokyo, Japan

21 **Read.** Talk and write.

How can you be on time?

I can ___get up early!_____

_____

_____

87

22 **Make an accordion book.**

1 Fold.

2 Write the day on the cover.

3 Write and draw on the pages.

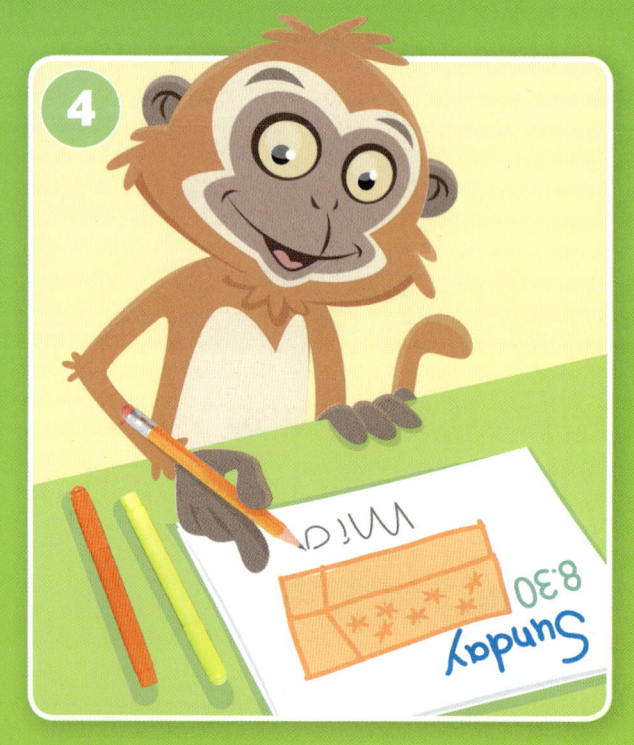

4 Write your name.

88

On Sundays I always get up at 8.30.

Now I can …
- ○ talk about what I do every day.
- ○ talk about when I do things.
- ○ name parts of the day.

89

Unit 6

How Are You?

In this unit, I will ...
- say how people look.
- talk about how people feel.
- talk about what people are doing.

Look and tick.

These children are
- ◯ happy.
- ◯ sad.

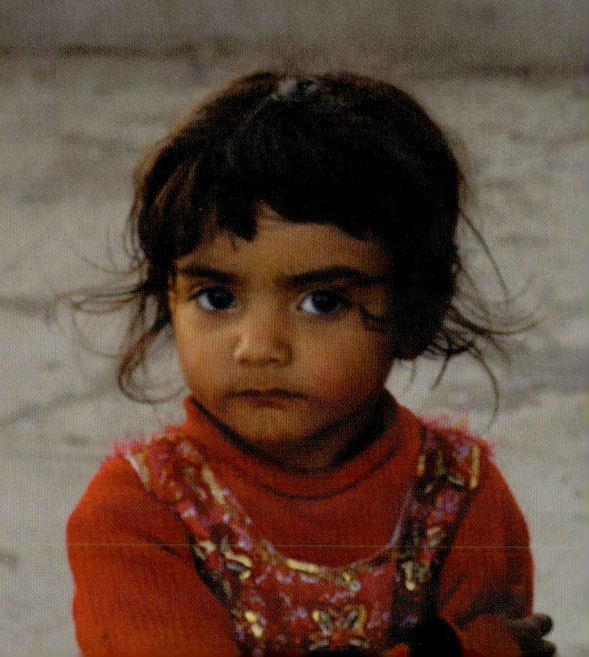

They are
- ◯ inside.
- ◯ outside.

Sana'a, Yemen

1 **Listen and say.** TR: B10

2 **Listen, point and say.** TR: B11

tired

scared

angry

excited

bored

92

3 **Work with a friend.** Ask and answer.

Is she scared?

No. She's surprised.

hungry

thirsty

worried

surprised

silly

93

4 **Listen.** Read and sing. TR: B12

Emotions

Sometimes, I'm happy.
Sometimes, I'm surprised.
Sometimes, I'm just silly.
I'm laughing inside!

Sometimes, I'm angry.
Sometimes, I'm just bored.
Sometimes, I'm excited.

How are you?
How do you feel?
How are you?
Tell me, please. How do you feel?

Sometimes, I'm smiling.
I'm laughing at a joke!
Sometimes, I'm crying.
I feel sad.

Sometimes, I'm tired.
Sometimes, I'm worried.
Sometimes, I'm feeling scared.

It's OK to feel sad,
but better to be happy.
It's OK to be silly,
or sometimes feel angry.

CHORUS

5 **Work in a group.** Take turns. Act out an emotion for your group to guess.

GRAMMAR TR: B13

How are you?

I'm **OK**. 😐   I'm **fine**. 🙂   I'm **great**! 😄

6 **Look.** Write questions and answers.

_____
_____

_____
_____
_____

_____
_____

7 **Listen.** Number the photos. TR: B14

96

GRAMMAR TR: B15

He **looks** worried.   No. He's tired.
She **looks** excited.   Yes. It's her birthday.

8 **Work with a friend.** Look and talk.

She looks scared.

No. She's worried.

97

9 Listen and say. Circle the letter. TR: B16

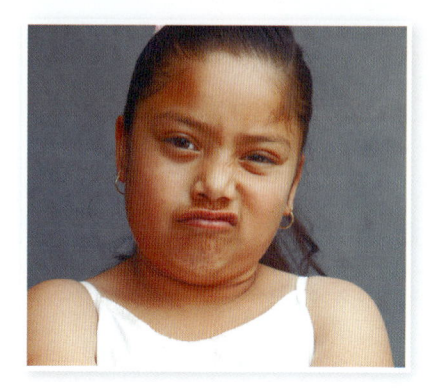

laughing

frowning

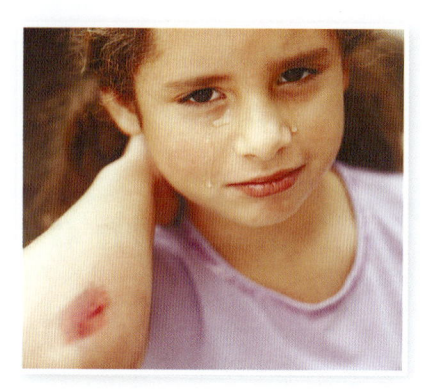

crying

smiling

yawning

1. The boy is   a. laughing.   b. smiling.
2. The girl is   a. crying.   b. frowning.
3. The girl is   a. yawning.   b. crying.
4. My sister is   a. smiling.   b. laughing.
5. My cat is   a. frowning.   b. yawning.

10 Work with a friend. Talk. Guess and stick.

This is a girl.

Is she smiling?

Yes. It's your turn.

1 2 3 4 5

GRAMMAR TR: B17

parent	**parents**	Our **parents** are taking us to the circus.
person	**people**	Some **people** don't like the circus.
child	**children**	Most **children** like the circus.

11 **Read and write.**

1. The ___students___ are smiling at the teacher. (student)

2. The _____ are laughing at the puppet. (child)

3. Some _____ are worried about the time. (person)

4. My _____ are angry about my untidy room. (parent)

5. Most _____ and _____ like sports. (boy/girl)

12 **Play a game.** Cut out the cards on page 167. Play with a friend.

This boy is worried.

That's right. My turn.

99

13 **Listen and read.** TR: B18

Fabulous Faces

People from all over the world paint their faces. Some people paint their faces to show how they feel about important days. For example, this Native American girl paints her face to show she feels proud of her community and traditions.

Others paint their faces to make people feel scared. Look at this man from India's scary, green face!

Lots of people paint their faces for fun, too. When some fans go to watch sports, they paint the colours of their team on their faces. They feel proud of their team.

In some places, people paint children's faces at parties. The children like having pictures of flowers, animals or characters from stories on their faces.

— North America

— India

Weird but true

People can make more than 10,000 different expressions with their faces.

100

14 Read and match. Draw lines.

1. This person has got an angry face.   Native American girl
2. This person is happy and proud.   man from India
3. They paint their faces at parties.   children

15 Read. Tick **T** for *True* or **F** for *False*.

1. The Native American girl feels proud of her community.   T F
2. The man from India paints his face because he feels sad.   T F
3. Sports fans paint their faces to scare people.   T F
4. Children paint their faces for fun.   T F

16 Read and tick. Why do people paint their faces?

	To feel proud	For fun
Children		
Sports fans		
You		

17 Talk. Work with a friend. Talk about face painting.

What do you want on your face?

I want a butterfly.

101

This is a photo of my birthday party. I am eight years old. You can see my parents and my friends in this photo. My friends are smiling. They are having fun. I am happy and I am very excited. I have got lots of presents! Look at my little sister. She is very happy, too!

18 **Write.** Choose a photo of you and other people.

1. What special day is it?

_____

2. Who are you with?

_____

3. How are the people feeling?

_____

19 **Work in groups of three.** Take turns. Read your writing to your group. Listen. Complete the table.

Name	Special day

NATIONAL GEOGRAPHIC

Our World

Be kind.

20 **Look and read.**

Help your friends and family.
Be kind to other people.

21 **Read.** Talk and write.

How are you kind?

I help my mum at home.

22 **Make a paper-bag puppet.**

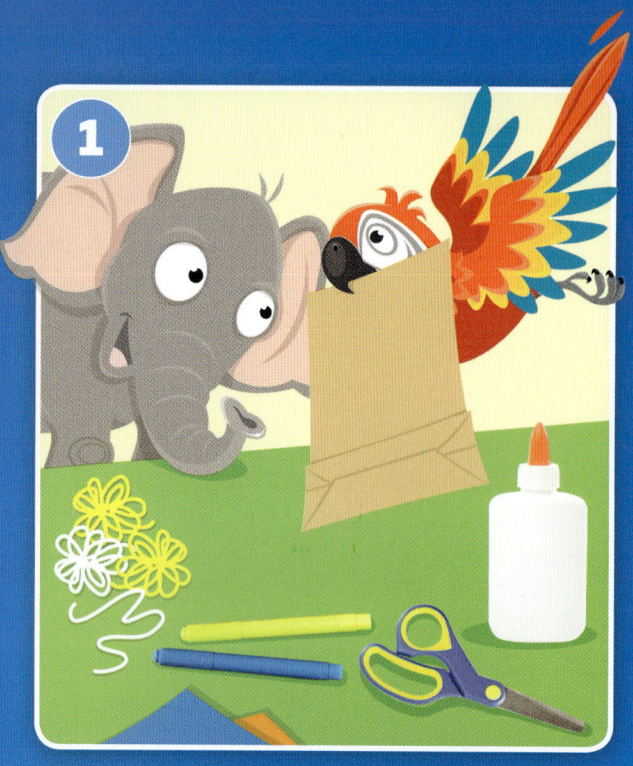

1 Use a folded paper bag.

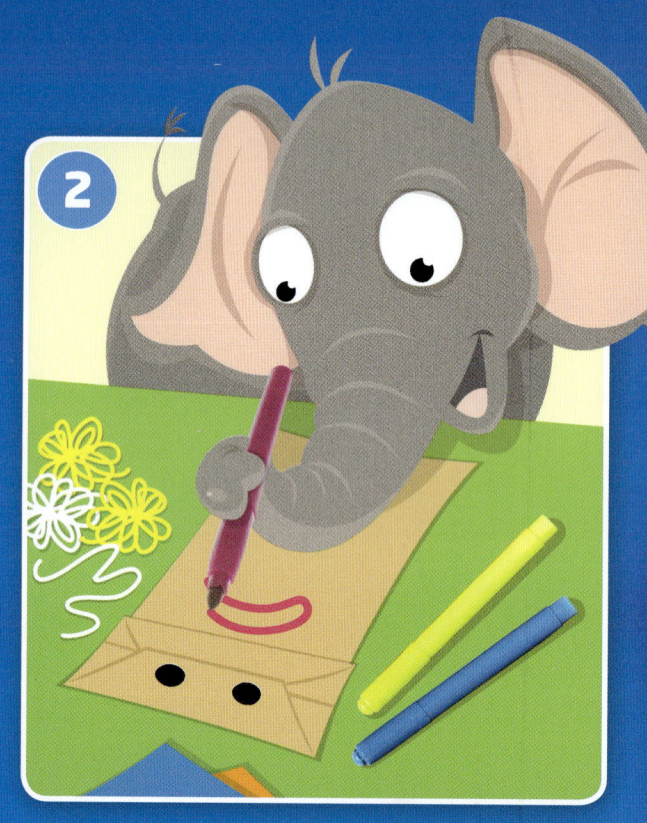

2 Draw a face. Glue shapes.

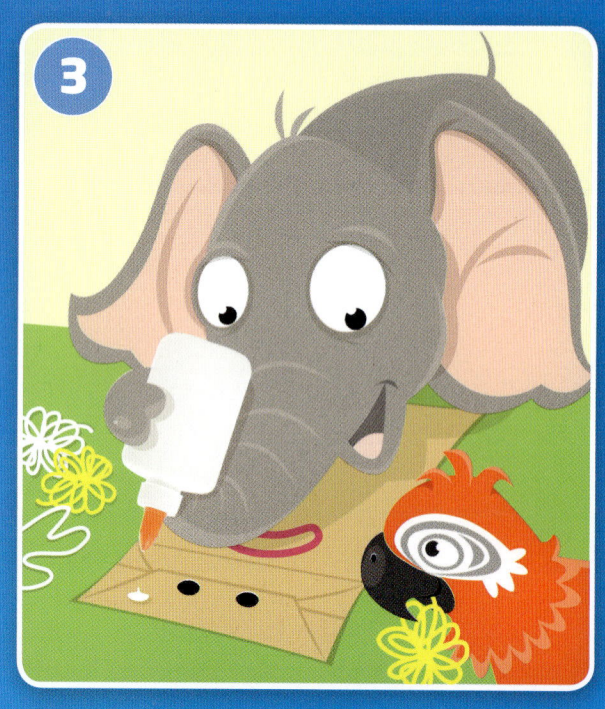

3 Glue on hair.

4 Decorate the clothes.

"This is my puppet. His name's Sam. He's sad."

Now I can …
- ○ say how people look.
- ○ talk about how people feel.
- ○ talk about what people are doing.

105

Review

You look worried. Miss a turn.

Start

Finish

106

How many yellow stars are there?

You're late for school. Go back one space.

Work with a friend.
Spin. Ask and answer.

When do you get up?

At 7 o'clock.

107

Unit 7

Amazing Animals

In this unit, I will …
- identify animals.
- describe animals.
- say what animals can and can't do.

Look and tick.

This animal is a
- ◯ fish.
- ◯ bird.
- ⊗ frog.

This animal can
- ◯ run.
- ⊗ jump.
- ◯ fly.

Red-eyed tree frog, Central America

109

1 **Listen and say.** TR: B19

2 **Listen, point and say.** TR: B20

a crocodile

a tiger

a lion

a zebra

a giraffe

a camel

a monkey

a panda

a parrot

a penguin

an elephant

a hippo

a kangaroo

swing

hop

3 **Work with a friend.** Ask and answer. Use these words.

| climb | fly | hop | jump |
| run | swim | swing | walk |

This animal can hop. What is it?

It's a kangaroo!

111

4 Listen. Read and sing. TR: B21

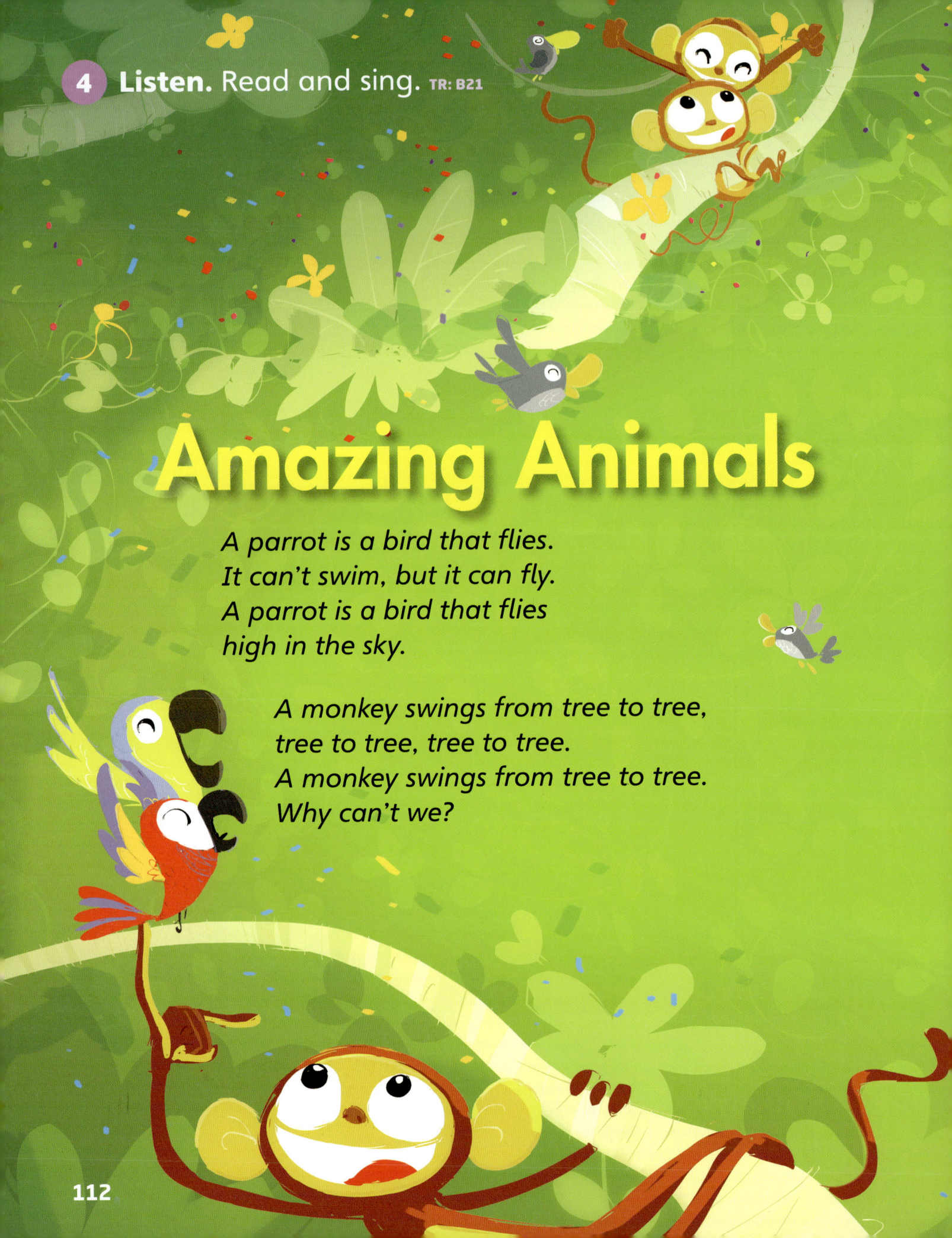

Amazing Animals

A parrot is a bird that flies.
It can't swim, but it can fly.
A parrot is a bird that flies
high in the sky.

A monkey swings from tree to tree,
tree to tree, tree to tree.
A monkey swings from tree to tree.
Why can't we?

I want to be a monkey in a tree.
I want to fly high up in the sky.

A penguin is a bird that swims.
It can't fly, but it can swim.
A penguin is a bird that swims
deep in the sea.

A kangaroo can hop and jump.
It can't climb, but it can jump.
A kangaroo can hop and jump
just like me!

I want to be a monkey in a tree!
I want to fly high up in the sky!
I want to be a monkey in a tree!
I want to fly high up in the sky!

5 **Work in a group.** Act out an animal for your group to guess. Take turns.

GRAMMAR TR: B22

A penguin **can** swim. It **can't** fly.
Penguins **can** swim. They **can't** fly.

6 **Read.** Write true sentences.

1. A hippo can climb trees.
   <u>A hippo can't climb trees.</u>

2. Zebras can't run.
   <u>Zebras can Run.</u>

3. A snake can walk.
   <u>A Snake can't Walk</u>

4. Elephants can hop.
   <u>Elephants can't hop.</u>

5. A crocodile can't swim.
   <u>A crocodile can swim.</u>

GRAMMAR TR: B23

Can a penguin swim? Yes, it **can**.   **Can** a penguin fly? No, it **can't**.
Can penguins swim? Yes, they **can**.   **Can** penguins fly? No, they **can't**.

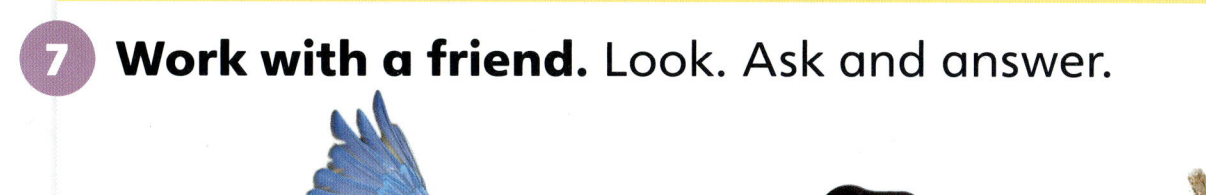

7 **Work with a friend.** Look. Ask and answer.

Can a lion jump?

Yes, it can.

115

8 **Listen and say.** Tick **T** for *True* or **F** for *False*. TR: B24

colourful feathers

sharp claws

a short tail

a long trunk

big teeth

1. Crocodiles have got colourful feathers. T (F ✓)
2. Elephants have got long trunks. T F
3. Pandas have got sharp claws. T F
4. Monkeys have got short tails. T F
5. Lions have got big teeth. T F

9 **Work with a friend.** Talk and stick.

Have hippos got long legs?

No, they haven't. They've got short legs.

short legs | long tails  | sharp claws  | long necks  | big ears

GRAMMAR TR: B25

Has a tiger **got** sharp claws?   Yes, it **has**.
Has a tiger **got** a trunk?   No, it **hasn't**.

Have tigers **got** sharp claws?   Yes, they **have**.
Have tigers **got** trunks?   No, they **haven't**.

10 Read and tick. Then listen to check your answers. TR: B26

	Big ears	Long neck	Sharp teeth	Long trunk	Colourful feathers	Long tail
Elephant	✓	✗	✗	✓	✗	✗
Giraffe	✗	✓	✗	✗		
Lion	✗	✗	✓	✗	✗	✗
Crocodile	✗	✗	✓	✗	✗	✓
Parrot	✗	✗			✓	✗

11 Play a game. Cut out the cards on page 169. Play with a friend.

Have giraffes got short necks?

No, they haven't. They've got long necks.

117

12 Listen and read. TR: B27

Two Big Birds

Cassowary

The cassowary is an amazing animal. It is big and strong and can live to be 60 years old. It lives in the rainforests in Papua New Guinea and Australia.

The cassowary can run really fast, but it can't fly. It can make loud noises, but it can't sing. Watch out! An angry cassowary can kick really hard!

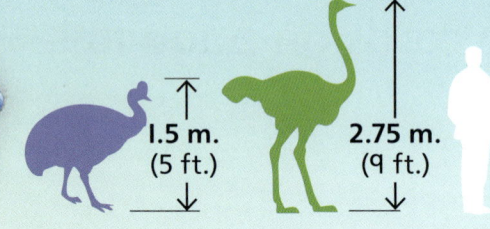

Ostrich

The ostrich is an amazing animal, too. It is very big and strong and can live to be 50 years old. It lives in the Savanna and Sahel areas in Africa.

Like the cassowary, the ostrich can run really fast, but it can't fly. It can also go without water for a long time. And yes, it can kick really hard, too!

1.5 m. (5 ft.)   2.75 m. (9 ft.)

Weird but true A male ostrich can roar like a lion.

13 Match. Join the sentence parts. Draw lines.

1. The cassowary and ostrich
2. The ostrich is
3. The cassowary is

a. very colourful.
b. can kick hard.
c. very tall.

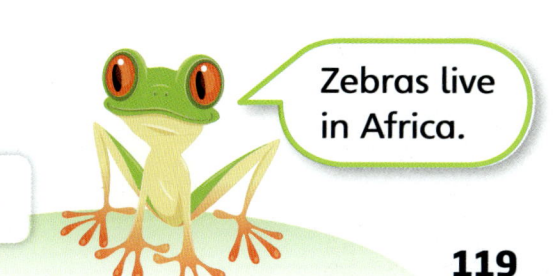

14 Look and read. Work with a friend. Talk about the birds.

Cassowary
- lives in Australia
- rainforests
- tall
- makes very loud noises

Cassowary and Ostrich
- can run fast
- can't fly
- can kick hard
- can live for a long time

Ostrich
- lives in Africa
- dry areas
- very tall
- goes without water for a long time

15 Read and write.

1. Can cassowaries make loud noises?

   _____

2. Can ostriches go without water for a long time?

   _____

3. Where do ostriches live?

   _____

4. Can cassowaries and ostriches fly?

   _____

16 Work with a friend. Talk about the animals.

camels   crocodiles   tigers   zebras

Zebras live in Africa.

119

My favourite animal is the kangaroo. It is a big animal with a long tail and strong legs. It can hop and jump. It can't walk or run. It has got a pouch for a baby kangaroo.
Lisa

17 **Write.**

Write about your favourite animal.

1. What is your favourite animal?

   _____

2. Describe your favourite animal.

   _____

3. What can your favourite animal do?

   _____

18 **Work in groups of three.** Take turns. Read your writing to your group. Listen. Complete the table.

Name	Favourite animal	What it looks like	What it can do

NATIONAL GEOGRAPHIC
Our World
Respect animals.

19 Look and read.

It is important to respect animals. Be kind and gentle.

Jane Goodall with chimpanzees

20 **Read.** Talk and write.
How can we respect animals?

We can _play with our pets._

_____.

We can be _____

_____.

play with
help

gentle
kind

121

21 **Make a class set of animal cards.**
Make a card about an animal.

1. Choose an animal.
2. Do research. 
3. Use pictures. 
4. Describe your animal.

Now I can …
- ◯ identify animals.
- ◯ describe animals.
- ◯ say what animals can and can't do.

Penguins are my favourite bird. They've got black and white feathers. They live in the ice and snow. They can swim, but they can't fly. Carla

My card is about penguins. They're really cool!

123

Unit 8
The World of Work

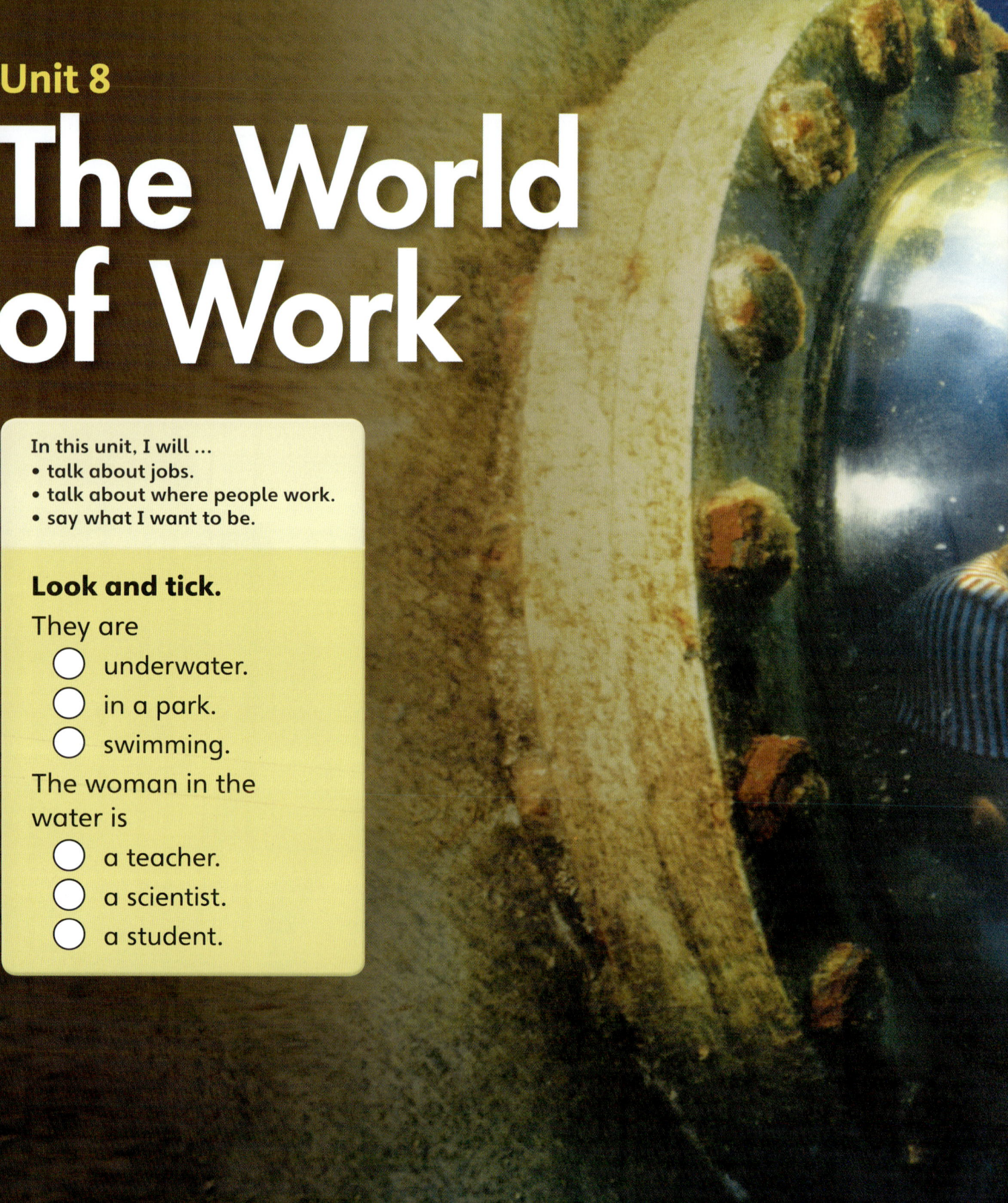

In this unit, I will …
- talk about jobs.
- talk about where people work.
- say what I want to be.

Look and tick.

They are
- ◯ underwater.
- ◯ in a park.
- ◯ swimming.

The woman in the water is
- ◯ a teacher.
- ◯ a scientist.
- ◯ a student.

Sylvia Earle working in an underwater habitat

1 **Listen and say.** TR: B28

2 **Listen, point and say.** TR: B29

a farmer

a vet

a doctor

a scientist

an office worker

a bus driver

a dentist

a police officer

a nurse

a firefighter

a singer

a chef

3 **Work with a friend.** Ask and answer.

He's wearing a hat.

Is he the firefighter?

No, he isn't.

He's the chef.

127

4 Listen. Read and sing. TR: B30

Work

What does your father do?
What does your mother do?
What does your brother do?
What do they do?

What does your father do?

He's a doctor. He's a doctor.
He's a doctor. Yes, he is!

I want to be a doctor!
I want to be a singer!
I want to be a rock star!
I want to be a farmer!
I want to be a dentist!
I want to be a chef!
I want to do it all!

CHORUS

What does your mother do?

She's a dentist. She's a dentist.
She's a dentist. Yes, she is!

CHORUS

What does your brother do?

He's a teacher. He's a teacher.
He's a teacher. Yes, he is!

What do you like doing?
What do you want to be?
What do you want to be?
Please tell me!

I want to be a doctor!
I want to be a singer!
I want to be a rock star!
I want to be a farmer!
I want to be a dentist!
I want to be a chef!
I want to do it all!

CHORUS

5 **Sing again.** Hold up pictures.

GRAMMAR TR: B31

What **does** your father **do**? He's a chef.
What **does** your mother **do**? She's a dentist.

6 **Listen.** Read and match. TR: B32

1. What does your mother do, Yong Soo?   a. He's a firefighter.
2. What does your aunt do, Lisa?   b. She's a singer.
3. What does your father do, Sofia?   c. She's a scientist.
4. What does your sister do, Ricardo?   d. He's a bus driver.
5. What does your uncle do, Ruby?   e. She's a nurse.

7 **Work with a friend.** Talk about what these people do.

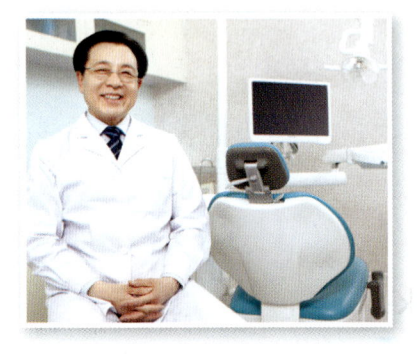

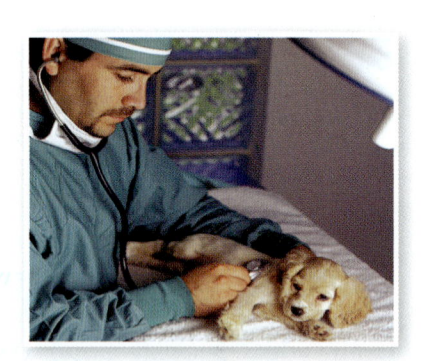

130

GRAMMAR TR: B33

| Where **does** your father **work**? | He **works** in an office. |
| Where **does** your mother **work**? | She **works** at home. |

8 **Look.** Ask and answer.

Where does your mother work?

She works in an office.

131

9 Listen and say. Look and write. TR: B34

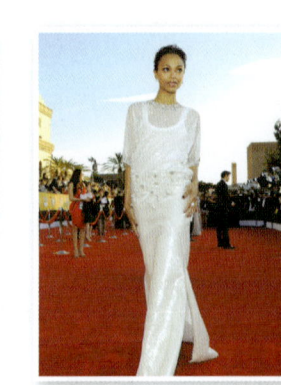

a rock star

a film star

an inventor

an artist

a football player

1. This person plays a sport. _She's a football player._
2. This person draws and paints pictures. _He's an artist._
3. This person sings to lots of people. _She's a rock star._
4. This person makes new things. _He's an inventor._
5. This person is in films. _She's a film star._

10 Listen and stick. TR: B35

GRAMMAR TR: B36

What **do** you **want to be** one day?
What **does** your brother **want to be**?

I **want to be** a film star.
He **wants to be** a doctor.

11 Read and write.

1. She loves animals. What does she want to be?
   A vet

2. She can sing very well. What does she want to be?
   A singer

3. She likes cooking. What does she want to be?
   A chef

4. He loves drawing and painting. What does he want to be?
   She is a film star

12 Play a game. Cut out the cube and the cards on page 171. Play in groups of six.

What do you want to be one day?

I want to be a chef.

133

13 Listen and read. TR: B37

Wonderful Work

Annie Griffiths is a photographer. It is a wonderful job. It is exciting and it is different every day.

Annie travels all over the world for her work. She takes photographs of people, places and animals. Sometimes, Annie's children go with her. Some photos have Annie's children in them.

She takes photographs of people at work and people having fun. She takes photos of cute animals and photos of very scary animals. She likes taking photos of places at night and in the morning.

Annie wants all her photos to tell a story. She wants people to think about them.

Life is an adventure for a photographer. Annie loves her job because she is always learning new things.

Weird but true

The first photo of a person is from Paris in 1838.

Victoria Falls, Zambia

1814 First photograph

1861 First colour photograph

1984 First digital camera

1999 First camera and video phone

14 Read. Choose and write.

> animals   bored   flowers   learning   photographer   story   vet

1. Annie is a _____.

2. She takes photos of people, places and _____.

3. She wants her photos to tell a _____.

4. Annie loves her job because she is always _____.

15 Work with a friend. Look and read. Talk about Annie's work.

Wants to:
tell a story
make people think

Job:
exciting
different

Photos of Places:
at night
in the morning

Annie Griffiths Photographer

Travels:
the world
with her children

Animals:
cute
scary

16 Work with a friend. Talk. Today you are a photographer. What do you want to photograph?

I want to take pictures of the mountains.

I want to take a picture of my family.

This is my Aunt Lily. She is a nurse. She loves her job. She works in a big hospital. At work, she wears a blue and white uniform and black shoes. My aunt likes helping people. In her job at the hospital, she helps sick people every day.

17 **Write.** Write about a person you know. Write about his or her job.

1. Who is the person? _____

2. What is his job? What is her job?

   _____

3. Where does he work? Where does she work?

   _____

4. What does he wear? What does she wear?

   _____

5. What does he do in his job? What does she do in her job?

   _____

18 **Work in groups of three.** Take turns. Read your writing to your group. Listen. Complete the table.

Name	Person	Job

NATIONAL GEOGRAPHIC

Our World

Work hard.

19 Look and read.

Work hard and enjoy your work.

Two young women, Myanmar

20 **Read.** Talk and write.
How do you work hard?

I _always do my homework._

21 **Make a poster about your favourite job and someone who does that job.**

1. Do research.
2. Choose a job.  
3. Draw and glue pictures. 
4. Write about the job.

He is my favourite artist and my favourite writer, too!

ARTIST

I want to be an artist. I love doing art at school. It's fun!
My favourite artist is Eric Carle. He makes children's books. He draws, he cuts paper and he glues it. His pictures are great!
Pedro

Now I can ...
- ○ talk about jobs.
- ○ talk about where people work.
- ○ say what I want to be.

139

Unit 9

Let's Eat!

In this unit, I will …
- talk about foods.
- say what I like eating.
- ask politely for things.

Look and tick.

This animal is
- ☒ small.
- ◯ big.

Its eyes are
- ☒ black.
- ◯ yellow.

It's
- ◯ eating.
- ◯ drinking.

Gecko, Hawaii

141

1 **Listen and say.** TR: B38

2 **Listen, point and say.** TR: B39

burgers

tomatoes

bread

sweetcorn

noodles

potatoes

142

mangoes

ice cream

carrots

pasta

beans

peppers

meat

3 **Work with a friend.**
Point. Ask and answer.

Do you like carrots and mangoes?

I like carrots, but I don't like mangoes.

4 Listen. Read and sing. TR: B40

Let's Eat!

Let's eat!
Do you like chicken?
Let's eat!
Do you like bread?
Let's eat!
Are there any carrots?
Let's eat!

Are there any mangoes?
Is there any cheese?
Is there any yoghurt?
May I have some, please?

Yes, there are mangoes.
Yes, there is some cheese.
There isn't any yoghurt.
Come and eat with me.

CHORUS

Is there any pasta?
Are there any beans?
Is there any meat?
May I have some, please?

Yes, there is some pasta.
Yes, there are beans.
There isn't any meat.
Please come and eat
with me.

CHORUS

I like chicken,
and you like beans.
Let's make a soup!

CHORUS

Let's eat!

5 **Work in a group.** Take turns. Play the food chain game.

Let's eat bread!

Let's eat bread and mangoes!

GRAMMAR TR: B41

Are there **any** tomatoes?	No, there aren't **any** tomatoes.
Are there **any** potatoes?	Yes, there are.
Is there **any** bread?	No, there isn't **any** bread.
Is there **any** milk?	Yes, there is.

6 **Look and listen.** Tick the food you need to buy. TR: B42

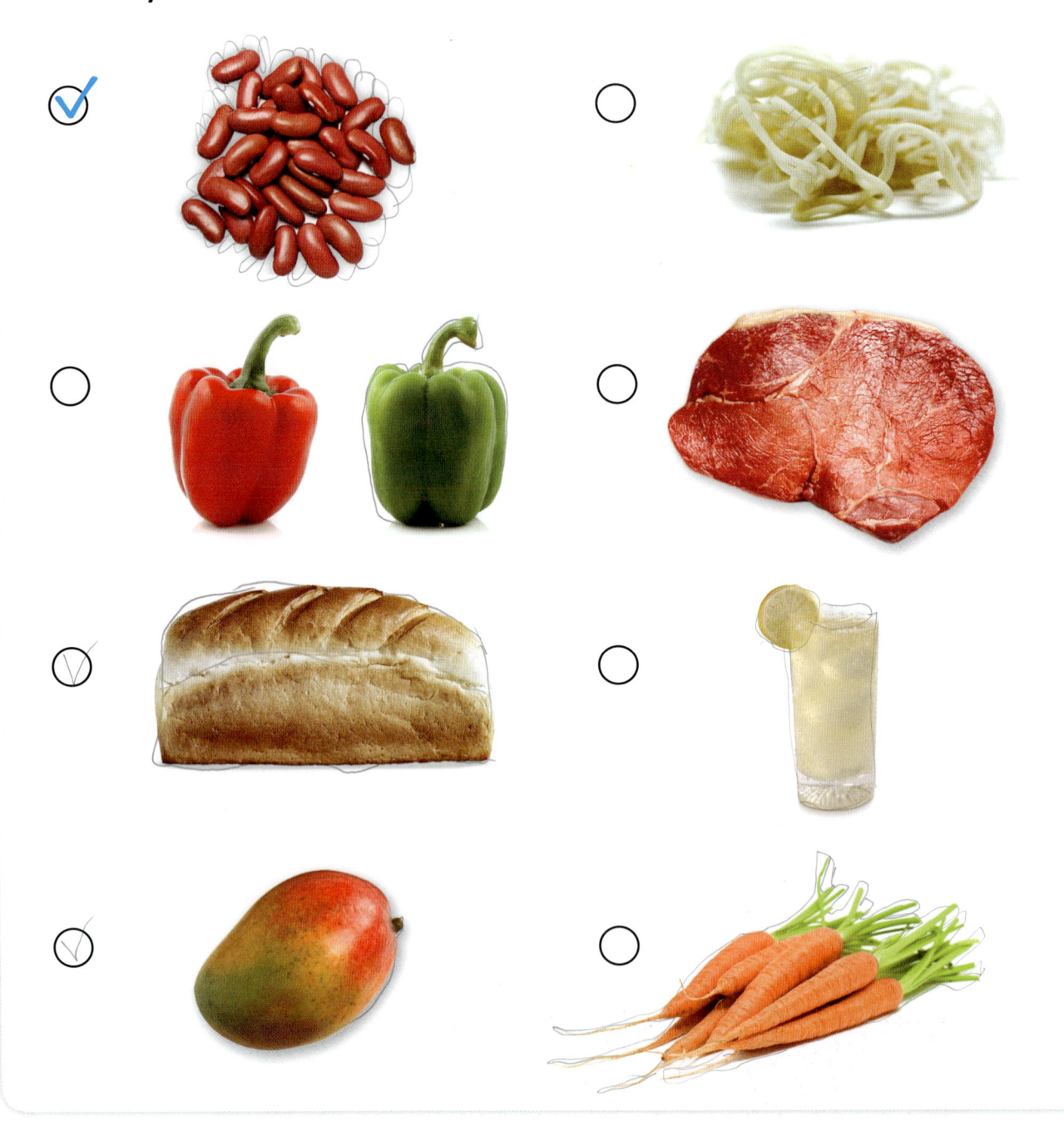

146

7 **Work with a friend.** Look. Ask and answer.

Is there any milk?

No, there isn't any milk.

Are there any burgers?

Yes, there are.

8 Listen and say. Look and write the letter. TR: B43

a grapes
b crisps 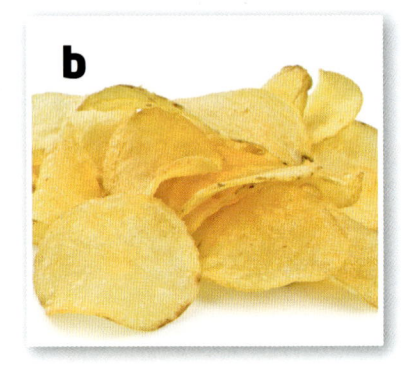 
snacks
c yoghurt
d nuts 
e cheese 

1. I eat crisps after school. _b_
2. My favourite snack is cheese. _e_
3. I like yoghurt for breakfast. _c_
4. I don't like nuts. _d_
5. Red grapes are delicious! _a_

9 Work with a friend. Talk. Guess and stick.

This is a boy.
Is he eating grapes?
No, he isn't.
Is he eating nuts?
Yes, he is!

GRAMMAR TR: B44

May I have some crisps, please?
May we have some pasta, please?

Not now. Dinner is at 7.00.
Yes, of course!

10 **Look.** Write questions.

_____

_____

_____

_____

_____

_____

_____

_____

11 **Play a game.** Cut out the gameboard and the pictures on page 173. Glue. Play with a friend.

B2. May I have some crisps, please?

Yes, here you are.

Sorry. I haven't got any crisps. C1. May I have some lemonade, please?

149

12 **Listen and read.** TR: B45

Super Snacks

People all over the world eat snacks. Fruit, crisps, nuts and sweets are popular. True, but what other kinds of snacks are out there? What other snacks do people enjoy?

Do you like fried butter or garlic ice cream? And what about ice cream with fish? You can eat these snacks in some parts of North America.

In some countries in Latin America, some people eat insects like ants, termites and grasshoppers. Roasted ants or grasshoppers make a delicious, crunchy snack.

And in some parts of Asia, some people like eating fried silkworms, water bugs and scorpions on sticks. They make a tasty snack, too.

Insects can also be a sweet snack. In Australia, people like eating honey ants. Their big stomachs are full of sweet juice. In other places, colourful lollipops with insects are popular. How about a sweet cricket, worm or scorpion lollipop?

The world is full of new and interesting food to try. It's snack time!

Weird but true

Cats can't taste sweet food.

13 **Tick T for *True* or F for *False*.**

1. Insects are popular snacks all over the world.   T   F
2. In Australia, honey ants are a popular snack.   T   F
3. In some places, you can get lollipops with insects inside them.   T   F

150

14 **Read and write.**

Super Snacks

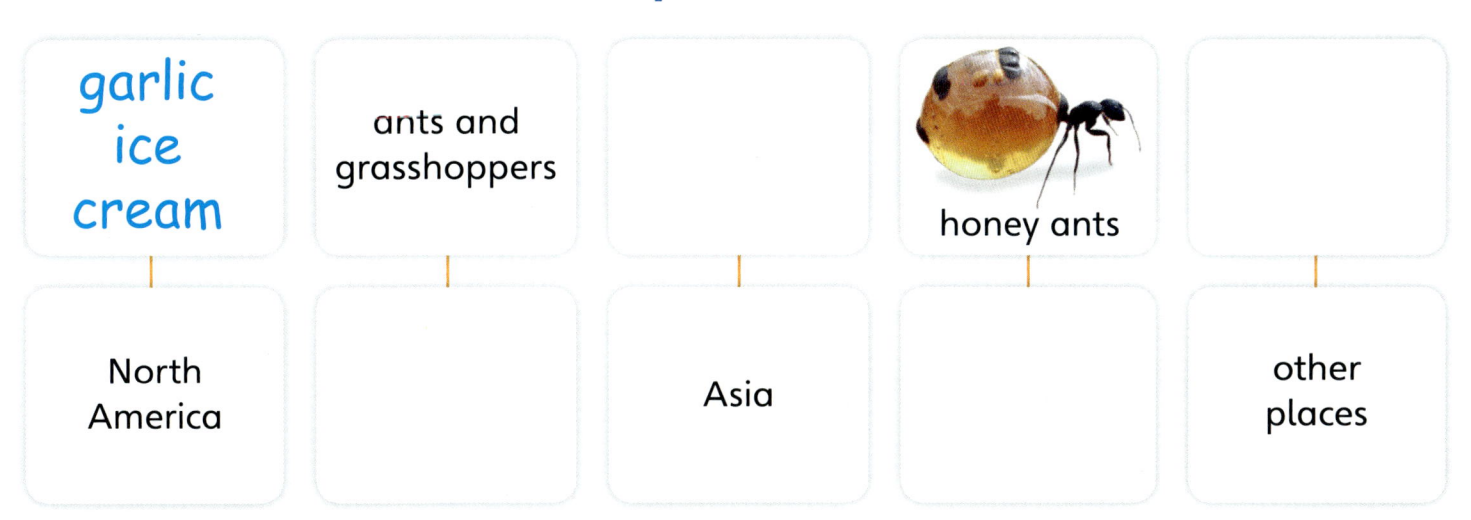

garlic ice cream	ants and grasshoppers		honey ants	other places
North America		Asia		

15 **Read and write.**

1. What snacks are popular around the world?

   _____

2. What do some people in some countries in Latin America like eating?

   _____

3. Where can you eat scorpion snacks?

   _____

4. What sweet snack do some people in Australia like eating?

   _____

16 **Work with a friend.** Name as many super snacks as you can.

My favourite snacks

I eat my snack at home after school. There are lots of snacks I like. Sometimes I eat fruit, nuts, yoghurt or cheese. At other times, I like eating crisps. And other times, I have a big mug of hot chocolate with biscuits or bread and butter. But my favourite snack is a lettuce, mayonnaise and peanut butter sandwich. Try it! It's delicious!

17 **Write.** Write about your favourite snacks.

1. When do you have a snack?

   _____

2. What are your favourite snacks?

   _____

3. How does your favourite snack taste?

   _____

18 **Work in groups of three.** Take turns. Read your writing to your group. Listen. Complete the table.

Name	Snacks

NATIONAL GEOGRAPHIC

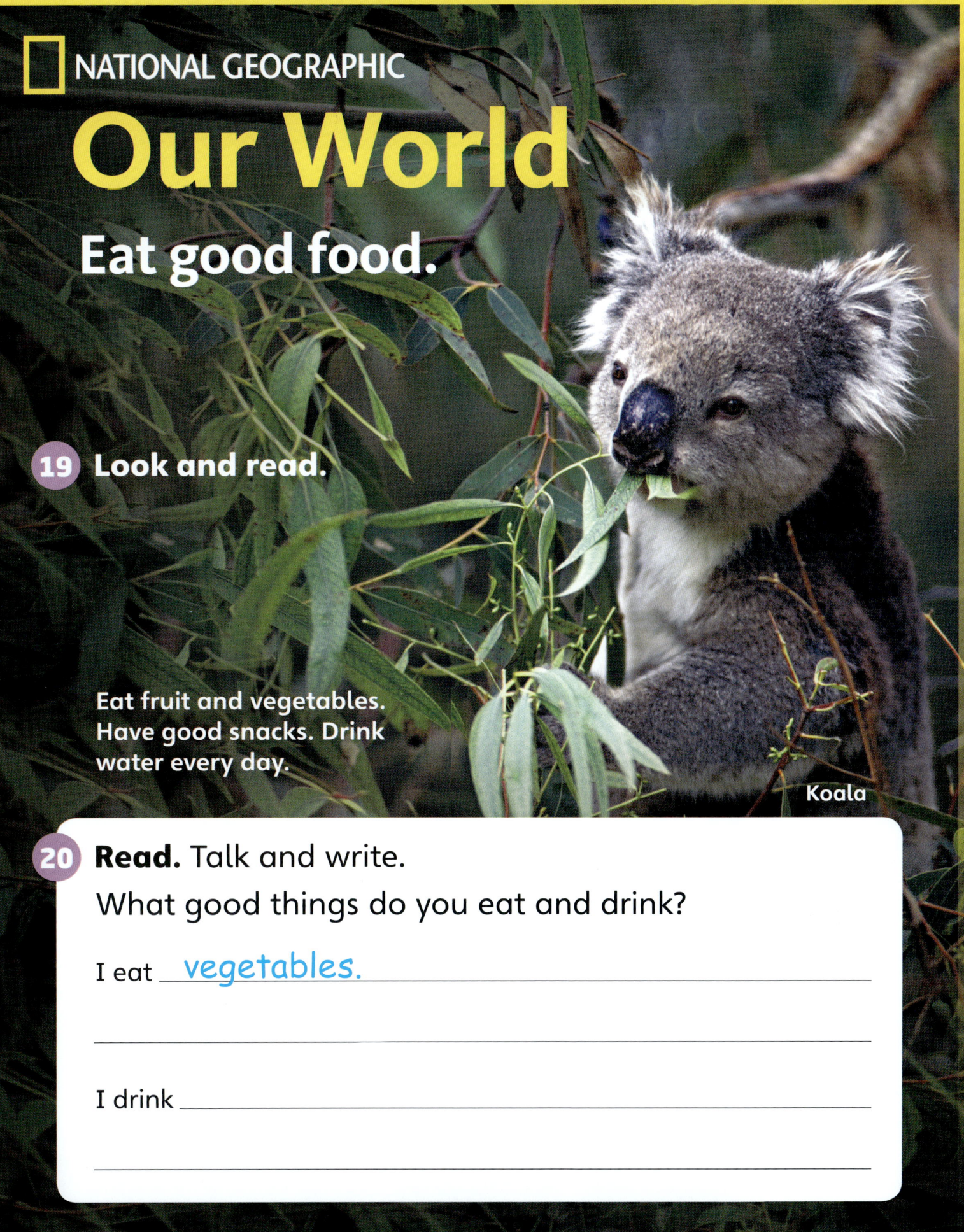

Our World

Eat good food.

19 Look and read.

Eat fruit and vegetables. Have good snacks. Drink water every day.

Koala

20 Read. Talk and write.

What good things do you eat and drink?

I eat _vegetables._ _____

_____

I drink _____

_____

21 **Make a class snack.** Follow this recipe.

1 Bring fruit and yoghurt to class.

2 Cut the fruit.

3 Put the yoghurt and fruit in a bowl.

4 Mix together.

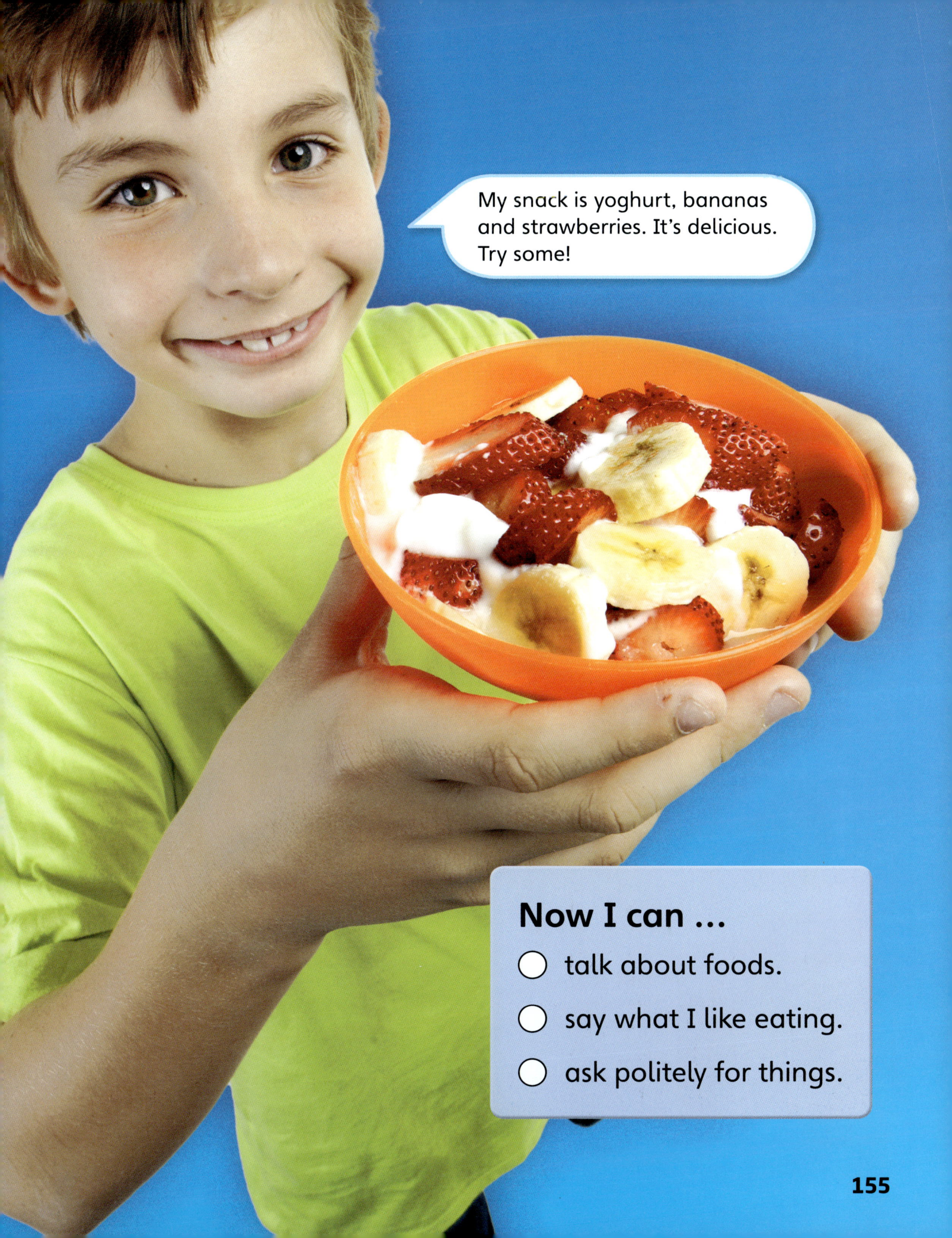

My snack is yoghurt, bananas and strawberries. It's delicious. Try some!

Now I can …
- ○ talk about foods.
- ○ say what I like eating.
- ○ ask politely for things.

Review

Start

Name four foods beginning with p.

Walk like a penguin.

156

You hide from a snake. Miss a turn.

Work with a friend. Spin. Ask and answer.

Are there any tomatoes?

No, there aren't.

Finish

157

NATIONAL GEOGRAPHIC OUR WORLD

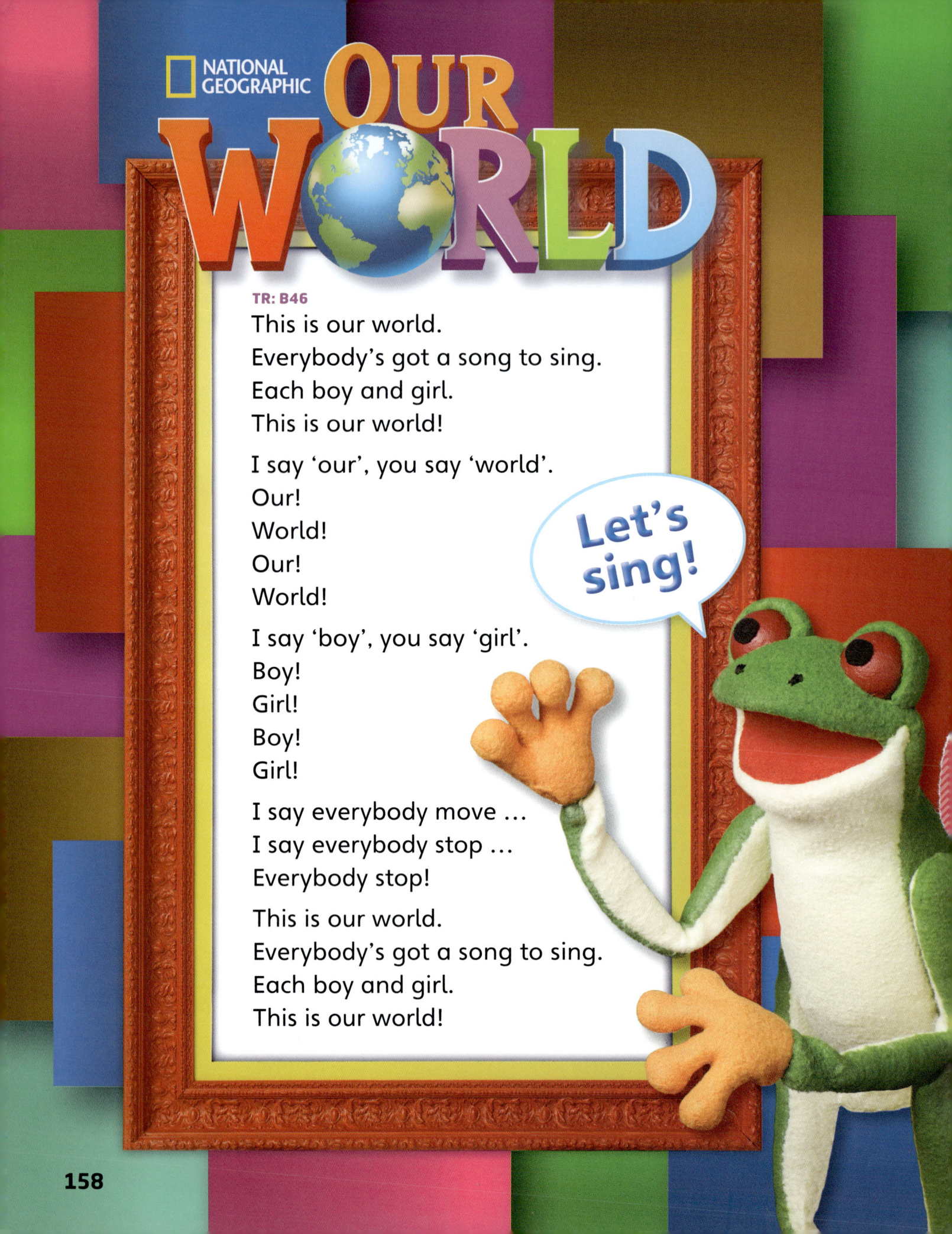

TR: B46

This is our world.
Everybody's got a song to sing.
Each boy and girl.
This is our world!

I say 'our', you say 'world'.
Our!
World!
Our!
World!

I say 'boy', you say 'girl'.
Boy!
Girl!
Boy!
Girl!

I say everybody move …
I say everybody stop …
Everybody stop!

This is our world.
Everybody's got a song to sing.
Each boy and girl.
This is our world!

Let's sing!

Unit 2 Cutouts Use with activity 12 on page 33.

161

Unit 3 Cutouts Use with activity 12 on page 49.

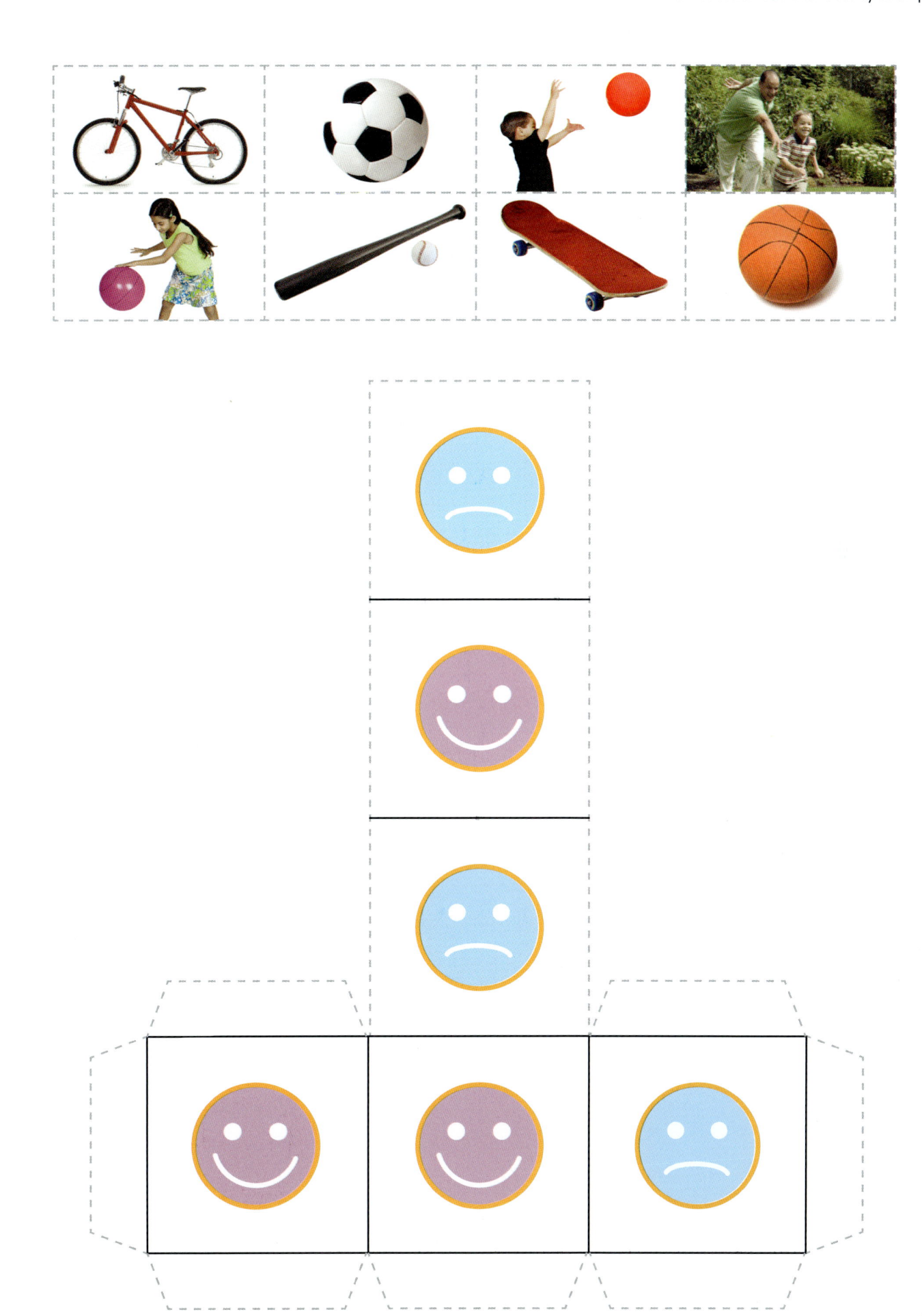

163

Unit 4 Cutouts Use with project on page 72.

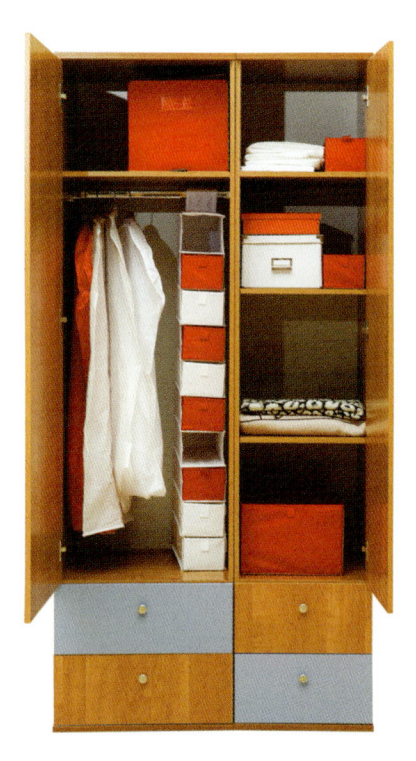

165

Unit 6 Cutouts Use with activity 12 on page 99.

| happy | worried | scared | laughing |

| excited | thirsty | yawning | hungry |

167

Unit 7 Cutouts Use with activity II on page 117.

169

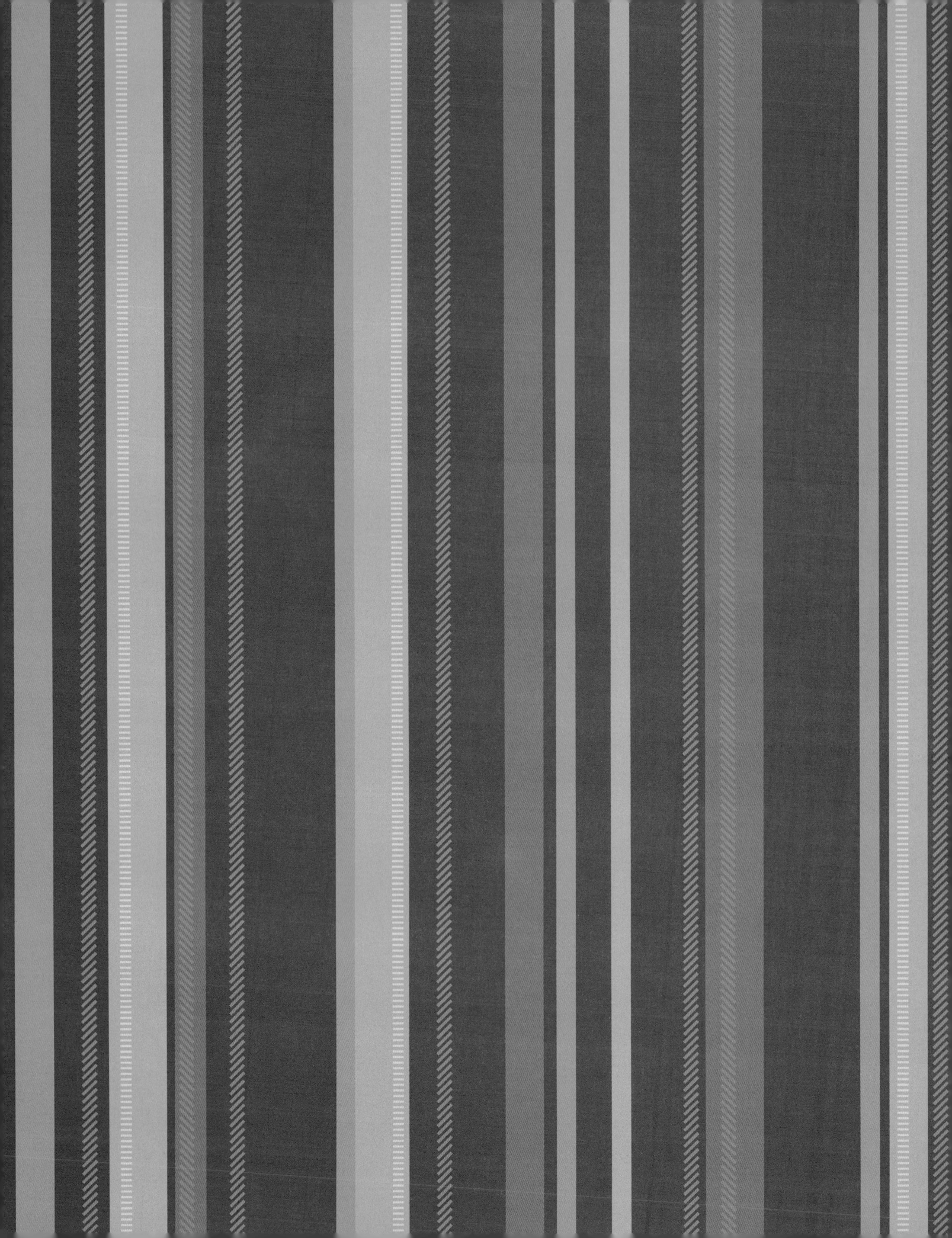

Unit 8 Cutouts Use with activity 12 on page 133.

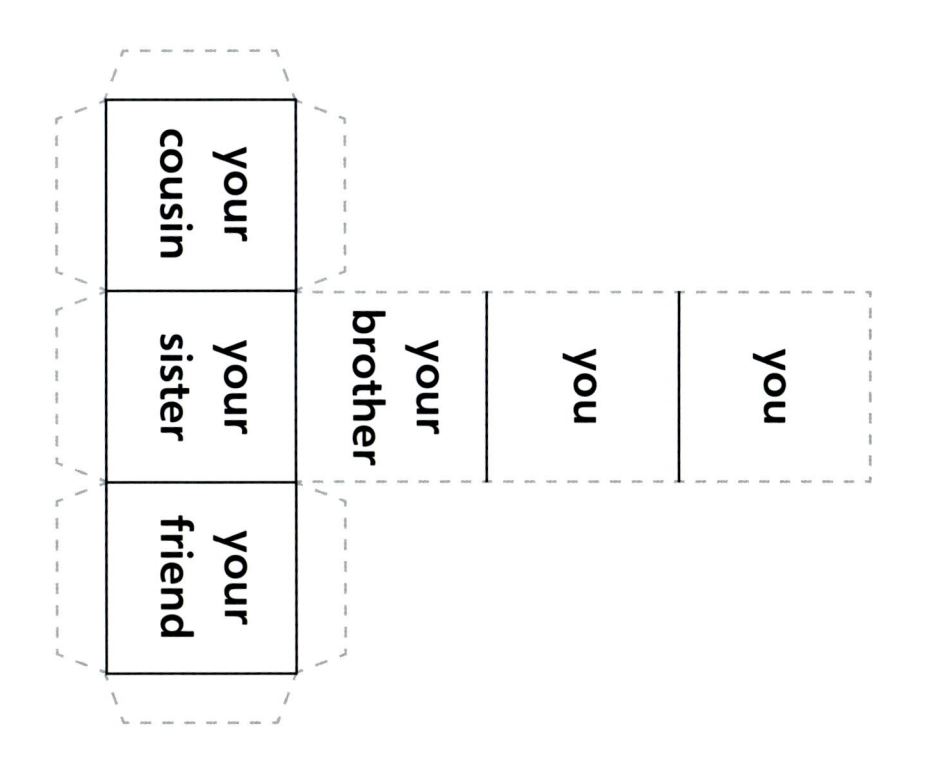

| your cousin |
| your sister | your brother | you | you |
| your friend |

171

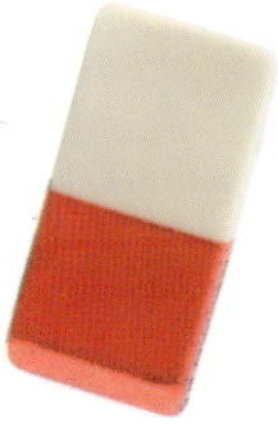

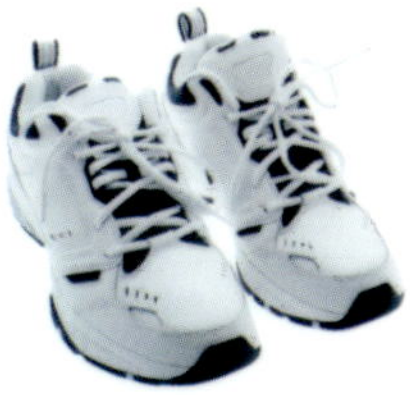
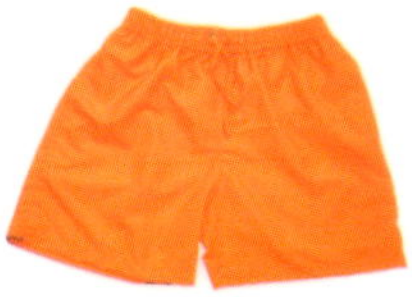
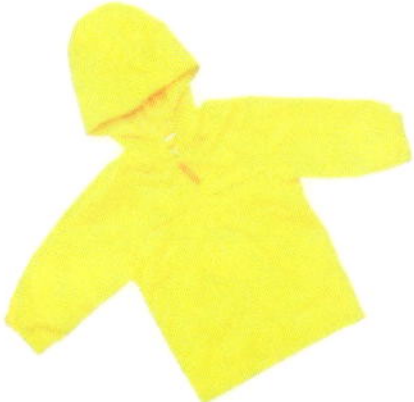
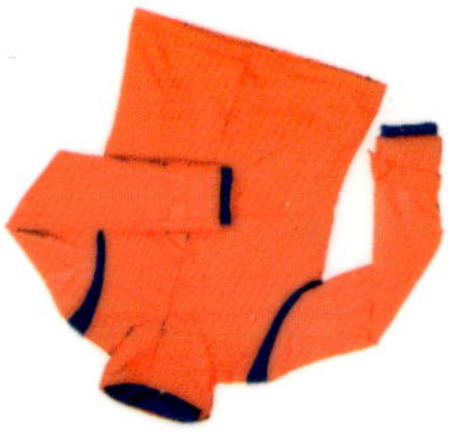
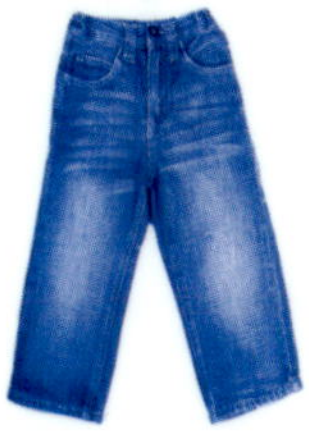
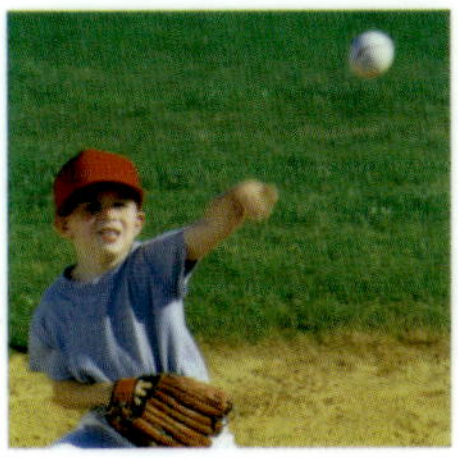
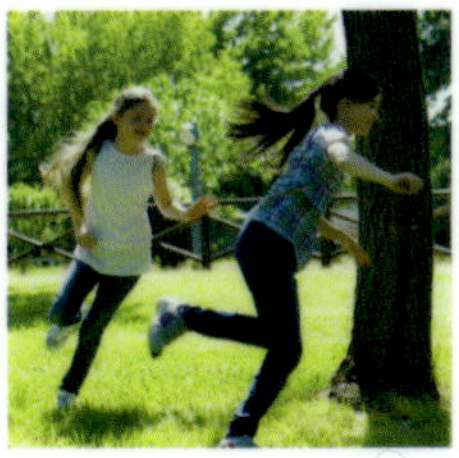
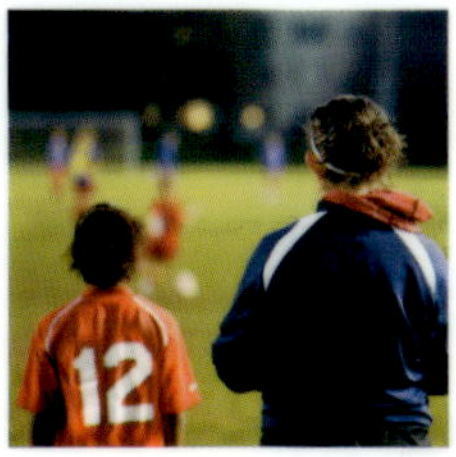
12
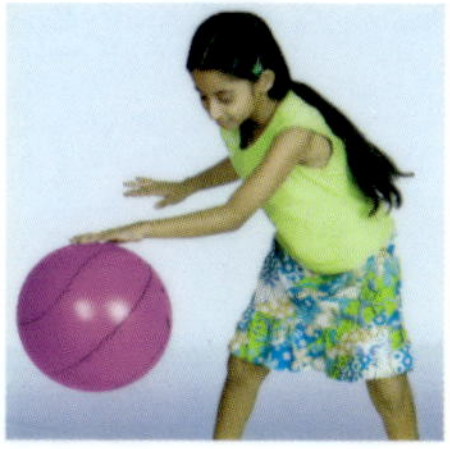
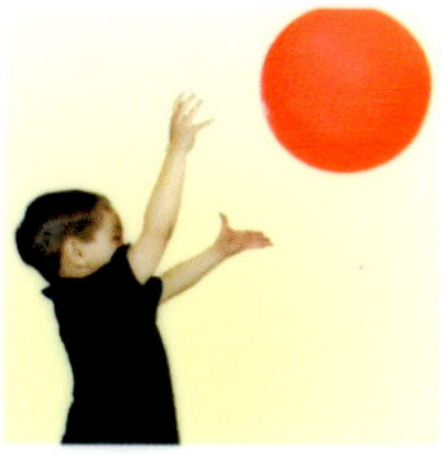

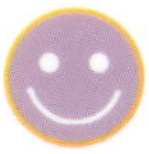

Unit 4 stickers

Unit 5 stickers

Unit 6 stickers

Unit 7
stickers

Unit 8
stickers

Unit 9
stickers

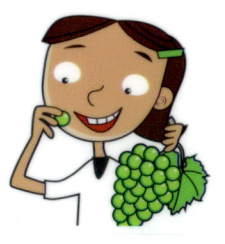